COMPOUNDING
THE
8TH WONDER

COMPOUNDING THE 8TH WONDER

Authored by
DEEPAK R. KHEMANI

penmanbooks.com

Penman Books

Office No. 303, Kumar House Building,
D Block, Central Market, Opp PVR Cinema,
Prashant Vihar, Delhi 110085, India
Website: www.penmanbooks.com
Email: publish@penmanbooks.com

First Published by Penman Books 2019
Copyright © Deepak R. Khemani 2019
All Rights Reserved.

Title: Compounding: The 8th Wonder
Price: ₹299 | $ 9.99
ISBN: 978-93-89024-63-0

No part of this book may be reproduced or transmitted in any form whatsoever, electronic, or mechanical, including photocopying recording, or by any informational storage or retrieval system without the expressed written, dated and signed permission from the author.

LIMITS OF LIABILITY/DISCLAIMER OF WARRANTY: The author and publisher of this book have used their best efforts in preparing this material. The author and publisher make no representation or warranties with respect to the accuracy, applicability or completeness of the contents. They disclaim any warranties (expressed or implied), or merchantability for any particular purpose. The author and publisher shall in no event be held liable for any loss or other damages, including but not limited to special, incidental, consequential, or other damages. The information presented in this publication is compiled from sources believed to be accurate, however, both the publisher and author assume no responsibility for errors or omissions. The information in this publication is not intended to replace or substitute professional advice. The strategies outlined in this book may not be suitable for every individual, and are not meant to provide individualized advice or recommendations.

The advice and strategies found within may not be suitable for every situation. This work is sold with the understanding that neither the author nor the publisher are held responsible for the results accrued from the advice in this book.

All disputes are subject to Delhi jurisdiction only.

Acknowledgment

This book would not have been possible without the help and support of each and every member of my family, My wife, VINISHA, Daughter DRISHTI, son RISHAAN, my dad RUPCHAND who at age 80 is fitter and more active than even me today, having been in Financial Services from 1963, till today almost all of what I know is learnt from him. Even today he personally meets all his clients, many of them 3rd generation, whom we are serving as Financial Planners, having helped them achieve their financial goals, and tries to help them in whatever way possible.

My earliest mentors, and now very good friends, Author Amit Trivedi, Author Vinayak Sapre, P V Subramanian of subramoney.com and Harish Rao. Mr. S R KOTI, from ABSL Mutual fund needs a special mention who has helped me in my journey of upskilling in Financial Education by arranging the CFGP and Advanced Financial Goal Planner certifications from AAFM(USA).

Hariharan and the entire team from the Edge Academy of Nippon Mutual Fund (earlier Reliance Mutual Fund) for the trainings to complete the NISM XA and XB Investment Advisor examinations and LIC of India for helping arrange the training for the Examination and Certification of Award in Financial Planning form CII(UK).

One of my RMs, Jigar Chhaya visited me 2-3 years ago in my office and said you should write a book, with the kind of experience and knowledge you have, it will be a great help to many people.

That thought stayed with me and in 2018, Surendran Jayashekhar of Success Gyan arranged a 3 day Book Writing boot camp where my book writing mentor Karan Hassija and Rajeev Talreja who took me through the step by step process of how to start writing a book right up-to its completion.

There are so many others who I may have missed out naming but I would like to thank all my friends and Family for being with me in this journey. This is not the first book I started writing but is the first one getting published and I can promise you It won't be the last!

Finally, a huge shout out to Tarun Singh and the entire team at Penman Publishing for working on the book, its title, the editing and getting it published and printed.

Preface

Deepak has phenomenal energy, his book Compounding The 8th Wonder is coming out. I've read the first chapter, it's going to intrigue you to read further, it's a phenomenal thing which he is writing about compounding.

If you're a teacher, a housewife, a carpenter, a car mechanic, if you're in business, if you're in a job, It doesn't matter what profession you are in, you got to have a copy of this book, to understand the Power of Compounding.

When you bring Compounding in your life, your life will go to a whole different level, most successful people do that.

He's bringing it out in such a simple fashion, even a 12-year-old can understand, what compounding can do for their lives. Check out his book, buy a copy, today right now.

Amandeep Thind

(Author, International coach, Speaker and Trainer at Brilliance Academy and Success Resources. He does the preview program, for Tony Robbins' Unleash The Power Within, in the UK, Europe and Asia. He is often referred to as the Tony Robbins of India)

Introduction

We have all heard about the 7 wonders of the world. There's a list of Seven Ancient wonders of the world

They were:

1. Great Pyramid of Giza, El Giza, Egypt.

2. Colossus of Rhodes, in Rhodes, on the Greek island of the same name.

3. Hanging Gardens of Babylon, in Babylon, near present-day Hillah, Babil province, in Iraq.

4. Lighthouse of Alexandria, in Alexandria, Egypt.

5. Mausoleum at Halicarnassus, in Halicarnassus, Achaemenid Empire, modern day Turkey.

6. Statue of Zeus at Olympia, in Olympia, Greece.

7. Temple of Artemis at Ephesus, in Ephesus (present-day Turkey).

In 2000 a Swiss foundation launched a campaign to determine the New Seven Wonders of the World. Given that the original Seven Wonders list was compiled in the 2nd century BCE—and that only one entrant is still standing (the Pyramids of Giza)—it seemed time for an update. And people around the world apparently agreed, as more than 100 million votes were cast on the Internet or by text messaging. The final results were announced in 2007.

They are as below

Rank	Wonder	Date of construction	Location
1	Great Wall of China	Since 7th century BC	China
2	Petra	100 BC	Jordan
3	Christ the Redeemer	Opened October 12, 1931.	Brazil
4	Machu Picchu	AD 1450	Peru
5	Chichen Itza	AD 600	Mexico
6	Colosseum	Completed AD 80	Italy
7	Taj Mahal	Completed c. AD 1648	India

However. when Albert Einstein, the world's greatest physicist and scientist says,

"*Compound interest is the eighth wonder of the world."*

He is not referring to any physical structure, ancient or new, its about compounding as a concept.

Let's see what has been said about Compounding by him and many other great thinkers, investors, leaders and influencers.

> "Compound interest is the eighth wonder of the world. He who understands it, earns it, he who doesn't, pays it."
>
> —Albert Einstein

> "Time is your friend, impulse is your enemy. Take advantage of compound interest and don't be captivated by the siren song of the market."
>
> —Warren Buffett

> "The strongest force in the universe is Compound Interest."
>
> —Albert Einstein

> "If you understand compound interest, you basically understand the universe."
>
> —Robert Breault

> "Understanding both the power of compound interest and the difficulty of getting it is the heart and soul of understanding a lot of things."
>
> —Charlie Munger

> "Good and evil increase at compound interest. That's why the little decisions we make every day are of infinite importance."
>
> —C. S. Lewis

> "Knowledge and productivity are like compound interest. The more you know, the more you learn; the more you learn, the more you can do; the more you can do, the more the opportunity."
>
> —Richard Hamming

"Most great fortunes are built slowly. They are based on the principle of compound interest, what Albert Einstein called, "The greatest power in the universe.""

—Brian Tracy

"The more we progress the more we tend to progress. We advance not in arithmetical but in geometrical progression. We draw compound interest on the whole capital of knowledge and virtue which has been accumulated since the dawning of time."

—Arthur Conan Doyle

"Read 500 pages every day. That's how knowledge works. It builds up like compound interest."

—Warren Buffett

"Compound interest is proof of gods existence."

—Jeff Rich

"I think people don't understand compound interest because typically no one ever explains it to them and the level of financial literacy is very low."

—James Surowiecki

"It should be everyone's right in a capitalist system to have some way to take advantage of compound interest."

—Katy Lederer

"Karma is an energy debt which you owe or an energy credit which is owed you. Both involve compound interest

that is added to the equation making it either
a burden or a blessing."

—Paul Russo

"Good and evil both increase at compound interest. That is why the little decisions you and I make every day are of such infinite importance. The smallest good act today is the capture of a strategic point from which, a few months later, you may be able to go on to victories you never dreamed of."

—C. S. Lewis

"It takes a long time to get good at something, so it's important to begin as early as possible so that we can improve and begin to see the compounding benefits of the work over time."

—Priscilla Chan

"Small, daily elevations compound into massive results over time."

—Robin S. Sharma

"The Compound Effect is the principle of reaping huge rewards from a series of small, smart choices"

—Darren Hardy

"Because we are always growing, life compounds and magnifies what is already in us. If you are miserable you grow in misery and if you are joyful you grow in joy."

—Bryant McGill

"Compound interest on debt was the banker's greatest invention, to capture, and enslave, a productive society."

—Albert Einstein

"All the benefits in life come from compound interest — money, relationships, habits — anything of importance."

—Naval Ravikant

Contents

Acknowledgment — v
Preface — vii
Introduction — ix

CHAPTER 1	What is Compounding	1
CHAPTER 2	The Story of the King, Poet and the Chess Board	7
CHAPTER 3	Our Introduction to Compounding	21
CHAPTER 4	Compound Interest	31
CHAPTER 5	Compound Interest The Story Continues	41
CHAPTER 6	Compounding Rules	49
CHAPTER 7	CAGR - Compounded Annual Growth Rate	57
CHAPTER 8	The 10,000 Hours	73
CHAPTER 9	Catalyst	83
CHAPTER 10	Habits Compound	93
CHAPTER 11	Negative Compounding	101
CHAPTER 12	Compounding in Nature	107
CHAPTER 13	The Rubiks Cube	115

CHAPTER 14	Compounding in Education	121
CHAPTER 15	Compounding in Life	125
CHAPTER 16	Compounding in Language	131
CHAPTER 17	Fastest Compounding in The World!	135
CHAPTER 18	Real Life Heroes Compounding	139

CHAPTER One

What is Compounding

"Compound interest is the 8th wonder of the world, he who understands it, earns it, he who doesn't, pays it. Compounding is the most powerful force in the universe"

I'm Sure many of us must have received or seen this quote on Social Media Platforms like WhatsApp, Facebook, Twitter etc. attributing it to ALBERT EINSTEIN.

Though there's some debate as to whether he actually said it or not, we'll leave that discussion for another day, let's try and understand the essence of what is being said and whether it really is a wonder as it is being made out to be.

Warren Buffet the most famous and quoted investor says "Over time compounding accomplishes extraordinary things"

What is the first thing that comes to mind when you hear the words "Power of Compounding?"

Money, Interest, Wealth, Stocks, Warren Buffett, Charlie Munger, Bitcoin, Art, Life, Growth, Progression, Success and many more.

Is Compounding only about these or is there more?

Let's do a search of the words "THE POWER OF COMPOUNDING" and see what results are displayed by Google

2,54,00,000 results in less than half a second, most of them related to Money, Finance, Life Insurance, Mutual Funds, Investments and more.

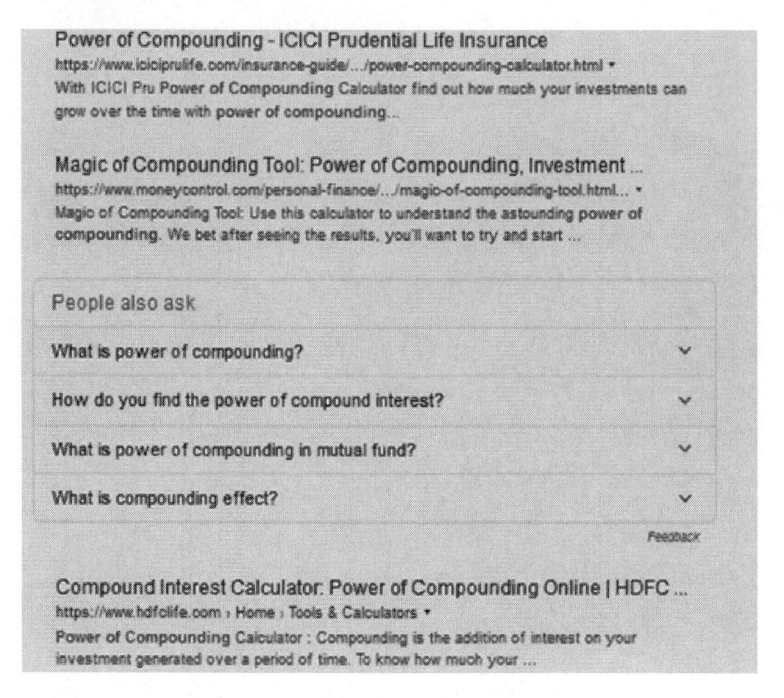

> **Power of Compounding - ICICI Prudential Life Insurance**
> https://www.iciciprulife.com/insurance-guide/.../power-compounding-calculator.html ▼
> With ICICI Pru Power of Compounding Calculator find out how much your investments can grow over the time with power of compounding...
>
> **Magic of Compounding Tool: Power of Compounding, Investment ...**
> https://www.moneycontrol.com/personal-finance/.../magic-of-compounding-tool.html... ▼
> Magic of Compounding Tool: Use this calculator to understand the astounding power of compounding. We bet after seeing the results, you'll want to try and start ...
>
> People also ask
>
> What is power of compounding? ⌄
>
> How do you find the power of compound interest? ⌄
>
> What is power of compounding in mutual fund? ⌄
>
> What is compounding effect? ⌄
>
> Feedback
>
> **Compound Interest Calculator: Power of Compounding Online | HDFC ...**
> https://www.hdfclife.com › Home › Tools & Calculators ▼
> Power of Compounding Calculator : Compounding is the addition of interest on your investment generated over a period of time. To know how much your ...

The Next Page Shows up These Results

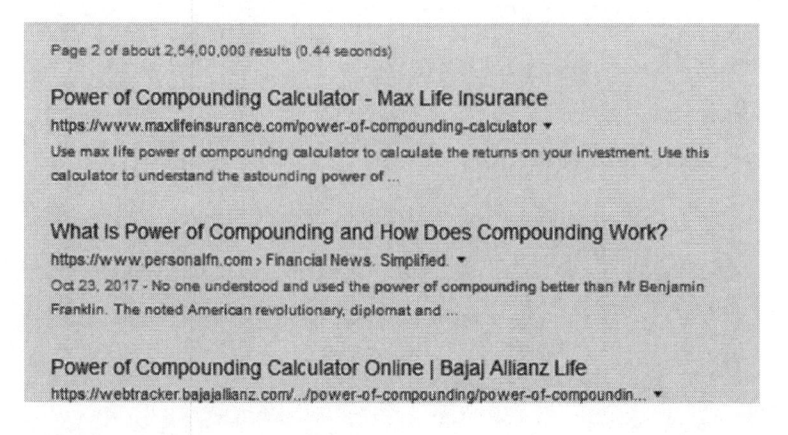

> Page 2 of about 2,54,00,000 results (0.44 seconds)
>
> **Power of Compounding Calculator - Max Life Insurance**
> https://www.maxlifeinsurance.com/power-of-compounding-calculator ▼
> Use max life power of compoundng calculator to calculate the returns on your investment. Use this calculator to understand the astounding power of ...
>
> **What Is Power of Compounding and How Does Compounding Work?**
> https://www.personalfn.com › Financial News. Simplified. ▼
> Oct 23, 2017 - No one understood and used the power of compounding better than Mr Benjamin Franklin. The noted American revolutionary, diplomat and ...
>
> **Power of Compounding Calculator Online | Bajaj Allianz Life**
> https://webtracker.bajajallianz.com/.../power-of-compounding/power-of-compoundin... ▼

Each and every page is about money, interest, wealth Investments, Insurance and so on.

Let's try and understand the power of compounding with an interesting story.

CHAPTER Two

The Story of the King, Poet and the Chess Board

The Story of the King, Poet and the Chess Board

A long time ago there was a King who had a lovely daughter, his only child, his princess, whom he loved very much. Everyone in the kingdom was fond of her as she was a very helpful soul, she was always happy and she saw to it that everyone in the kingdom stayed happy. However, since a few days, due to some reason, she had become very sad. The king tried finding out but couldn't. She had stopped smiling, talking to others and the king had tried everything he could to make her happy, but failed.

So, one day he sent out a message in his kingdom; If anyone can make my daughter laugh, I will reward that person, with whatever he asks.

Many people, like the court jester, some clowns from the circus, the king's ministers, and others, from neighboring kingdoms, tried their luck to make the princess laugh with different tricks but they failed! Nobody could even make the princess to smile!

Far away in the jungle at the outskirts of the kingdom, lived a poet with his family, his wife came to know about this announcement from the king and she told the poet, we are going through difficult times financially, you are a poet, you write poems that are sarcastic and funny, why don't you try your luck at making the princess laugh?

If you succeed the king will give you whatever you ask and our family will be able to lead a good life. The poet agreed and went to the palace where the King was seated with his ministers and his subjects, and he announced,

Your Majesty, I am here to make the Princess laugh, I may be given a chance!

So many people had tried before him and the king had almost given up, thinking my daughter will never be happy again, however he reluctantly agreed.

The poet then went on to read out a very funny poem of his and as soon as the princess heard it, she started laughing.

Everyone seated in the palace were overjoyed, The King walked down to the poet, hugged him and said, you have made my princess laugh, ask whatever you want and it will be given, your wish is my command!

The poet asked, my respected King will you really give me whatever I ask?

The King said Yes, I am the King, ask and you shall be rewarded with whatever you want. I can give you money, gold ornaments, precious jewelry, animals, land whatever you want!

The poet said I do not want any money or gold ornaments or any valuables, all I want is this,

Bring a chess board, put ONE grain of rice on the first square and I want you to keep on doubling it every square, so there's 2 grains of rice on the 2nd, 4 on the 3rd, 8 on the 4th, 16 on the fifth and so an till you reach the 64th square. If you agree to this, I will consider myself rewarded.

Everyone who was seated in the Palace was Surprised, including the King, He asked the poet, are you sure? You want grains of rice doubling every square!

I'm ready to give you whatever you want, money, gold coins, Jewelry, horses, cows, land anything, I can give you my daughter's hand if you ask for it, but want grains of rice!

Yes, my Respected king, the poet said, that's exactly what I want.

The king and his ministers who were seated in the Palace thought, this poet is a fool, He could have asked for whatever he wanted and all he wants is grains of rice. The king ordered his food minister to open the gates of the granary and give the poet all the grains of rice as per his wish.

They started as the poet had asked, with 1 grain of rice in the first square and then doubling every square, so, they put 2 on the 2nd square, 4 on the 3rd and so on.

12 *Compounding: The 8th Wonder*

By the time they reached the 10th square they had to put 512 grains of rice.

Slowly, Square by Square the number of Grains needed, kept on Doubling!

By the time they reached the 20th square the number of grains was 5,24,288

By the time they could reach the halfway mark the 32nd square needed 214,74,83,648 grains of rice! (214 crores 74 lakhs 83 thousand six hundred and 48)

Soon the count increased to lakhs of crores. They had run out of stock of all the rice they had in their granary.

They called for stock of rice from neighboring kingdoms however that too got finished in a few squares. There was no more stock of Rice anywhere!

The King and all the ministers who were laughing, on the poet when he put his request of rice grains as his reward, were astonished to see what was happening! The Food Minister came and told the king that it was impossible to fill all the squares with grains of Rice as they had promised.

Eventually the king walked down and with folded hands, fell on the poet's feet and said I am unable to fulfill my promise, you can take my entire kingdom if you want, but I have no more rice to give you!

Of course, the poet did not take the kingdom as that was not his intention, he said My respected King, I live far away in the jungle, all I need a permanent job in your palace so that my family can lead a comfortable life.

He said, I just wanted you to appreciate and understand the power of compounding. The king immediately agreed and gave him the responsibility of two very important portfolios.

He appointed him as the finance minister and the education minister of his kingdom from that day onwards. Education Minister because the king realized that this very important concept of Compounding was not being taught in schools, it is very important for children to learn and understand the concept of compounding early on in their life and also the finance minister because compounding affect finances, a lot!

Wouldn't you like to know how many grains would have been required on the 64th square?

It's a number which is difficult to comprehend.

Its 19 digits, It is 9,22,33,72,036,85,47,75,808

It is NINE Quintillion, Two hundred and Twenty-Three Quadrillion, Three Hundred and Seventy-Two Trillion, Thirty-Six Billion, Eight Hundred and Fifty-Four Million, Seven Hundred and Seventy-Five Thousand Eight Hundred and Eight only!

Also remember if 64th Square had 9 quintillion, the 63rd would have 4.5 Quintillion grains and the 62nd would have 2.25 quintillion!

It impossible to even imagine such large numbers when doing a calculation!

The table below shows how many grains of rice would have been needed on each square!

Square	Number of Grains
1	1
2	2
3	4
4	8
5	16
6	32
7	64

Compounding: The 8th Wonder

Square	Number of Grains
8	128
9	256
10	512
11	1,024
12	2,048
13	4,096
14	8,192
15	16,384
16	32,768
17	65,536
18	131,072
19	262,144
20	524,288
21	1,048,576
22	2,097,152
23	4,194,304
24	8,388,608
25	16,777,216
26	33,554,432
27	67,108,864
28	134,217,728
29	268,435,456
30	536,870,912
31	**1,073,741,824**
32	2,147,483,648
33	4,294,967,296
34	8,589,934,592
35	17,179,869,184

Square	Number of Grains
36	34,359,738,368
37	68,719,476,736
38	137,438,953,472
39	274,877,906,944
40	549,755,813,888
41	1,099,511,627,776
42	2,199,023,255,552
43	4,398,046,511,104
44	8,796,093,022,208
45	17,592,186,044,416
46	35,184,372,088,832
47	70,368,744,177,664
48	140,737,488,355,328
49	281,474,976,710,656
50	562,949,953,421,312
51	1,125,899,906,842,624
52	2,251,799,813,685,248
53	4,503,599,627,370,496
54	9,007,199,254,740,992
55	18,014,398,509,481,984
56	36,028,797,018,963,968
57	72,057,594,037,927,936
58	144,115,188,075,855,872
59	288,230,376,151,711,744
60	576,460,752,303,423,488
61	1,152,921,504,606,846,976
62	2,305,843,009,213,693,952
63	4,611,686,018,427,387,904

Square	Number of Grains
64	9,223,372,036,854,775,808

This, my dear readers, is just one example of how Powerful Compounding is!

NO WONDER COMPOUNDING IS CALLED
THE 8th WONDER
COMPOUNDING IS POWERFUL
COMPOUNDING TAKES TIME

Let's take another example

I'll ask you a simple question!

If I told you I'll give you Rupees 1 crore (10 Million) today or I'll give you one Rupee which doubles everyday for the next 31 days what will you take, without using a calculator!

Most people will take the One crore, or the 10 Million.!

However, you, my dear readers are smart, you have now read the story of the King, the poet and the chessboard and you now understand how compounding works!

Many of you will now say I'll take the one Rupee doubling every day for 31 days, without actually knowing how much it will actually become!

To see how much, it will actually become, do refer to the previous table at square No 31, which I'm sure some of you may have already, it's highlighted.

It will be 100 Crore on the 31st day. The actual number

is 1,07,37,41,824

One Hundred and Seven Crore 37 Lakh Forty-One Thousand Eight Hundred and Twenty-Four!

That's Compounding for You, The Miracle of Compounding Returns!

NO WONDER COMPOUNDING IS THE 8th WONDER OF THE WORLD

COMPOUNDING IS POWERFUL, COMPOUNDING TAKES TIME

CHAPTER
Three

Our Introduction to Compounding

Whhen were we first introduced to the concept of Compounding?

I remember, in school sometime in the 6th or the 7th Standard we were introduced to the Formula of Compound Interest in our Mathematics Class.

$$A = P\left(1 + \frac{r}{n}\right)^{nt}$$

Where,

- P = principal amount (initial investment)
- r = annual nominal interest rate (as a decimal)
- n = number of times the interest is compounded per year
- t = number of years

How many of us even remember this formula? For those of us who do remember, are we using it in day to day life? For most of us the answer is, no!

We were given a few problems to solve in our Mathematics class where a few variables were given and we had to find the answer of the one whose value was not available, Right!

We were all interested in passing the exams, most of us forget about it in a few months or a few years except for those who went on to study higher Mathematics in Engineering maybe.

However even before this formula of compounding was taught to us, in the Mathematics class, the word compound was introduced to us, earlier!

I want you to go back, a little earlier, in your school days to your Chemistry class.

Our Introduction to Compounding 25

That was the first time when we heard the word COMPOUND in School.

Let's see the dictionary meaning of the word **Compound.**

Something that is made up of 2 or more unique elements, to combine together so as to form a whole, consisting of two or more substances, ingredients, elements, or parts.

Example:

Water is a compound, a single molecule of water has 2 atoms of Hydrogen and 1 atom of Oxygen.

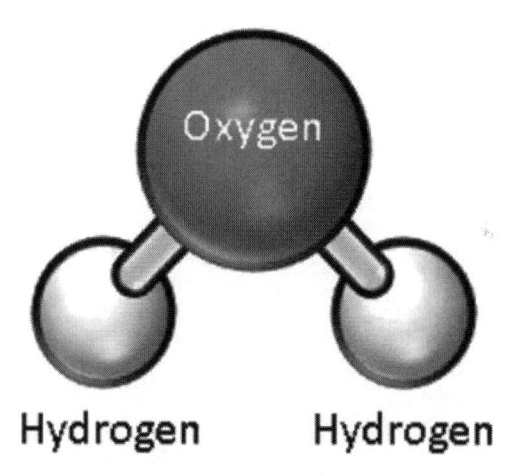

Oxygen

Hydrogen Hydrogen

The water we drink, if it was only one element, hydrogen or oxygen, it would be undrinkable!

Table Salt, or Common Salt which we use daily in our food is a compound, one part each of Sodium and Chlorine

26 Compounding: The 8th Wonder

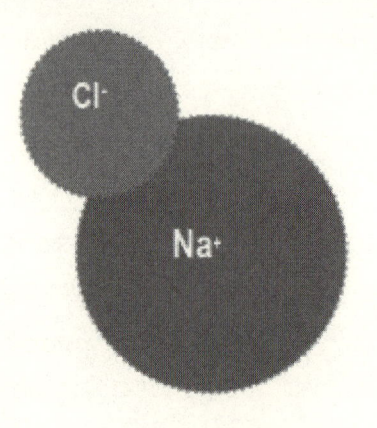

Salt (NaCl)

What if we added only Sodium or Chlorine to our food!

Would we be able to eat it?

The air we breathe has Nitrogen, Oxygen, Carbon Dioxide, and other gases.

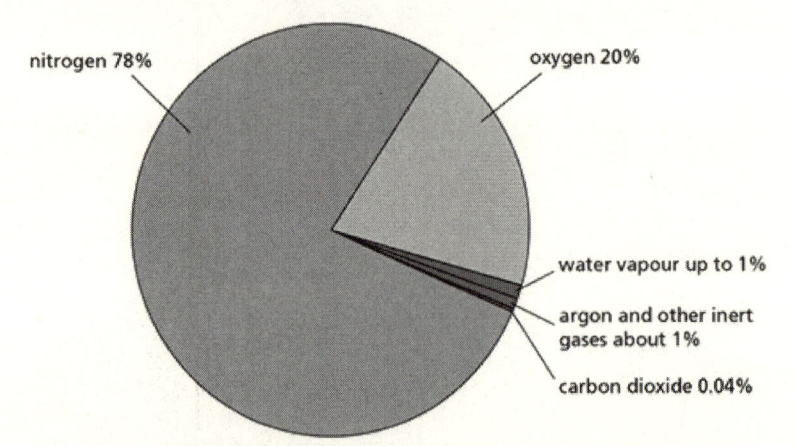

- nitrogen 78%
- oxygen 20%
- water vapour up to 1%
- argon and other inert gases about 1%
- carbon dioxide 0.04%

If air had only Oxygen, we would have all burnt up by now!

If the air was only Nitrogen, or Carbon Dioxide we would have all suffocated to death!

The food we eat is a compound, Dal Rice, Vegetable Paratha, Chhole Bhature and so on,

Even as I'm writing this my mouth is watering!

Imagine eating only rice, or wheat or jowar or a single vegetable, without salt, pepper, spices and herbs! Would we be able to eat, would we even call it food!

In fact, almost everything that touches us in life, everything that we do, we eat, we talk, we read, we learn, is either a result of compounding or an effect of compounding.

When I started writing this chapter, I realized that I had come across the word compound much earlier.

The word I'm referring to is "COMPOUNDER"

I'm sure some of you would have got a hint by now.

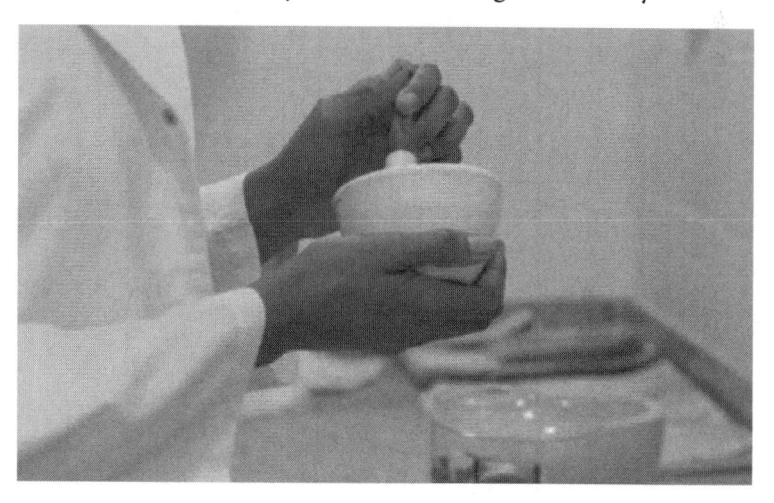

As a child, growing up, whenever we used to go to see our Family doctor for any health issue like a fever, cough, or a cold, the doctor used to check us and write out a prescription. That would then be handed over to his helper, his assistant, called the COMPOUNDER.

A *compounder* is a person who mixes up the ingredients and prepares the medicine and also hands it off to the patient.

This person used to take out the tablets prescribed by the doctor and typically show us 3 different colored tablets to be taken 3 times a day!

3 Different tablets to be taken at a time, Remember the dictionary definition of compounding we mentioned at the start. A minimum of 2 different elements. Here it was 3 different tablets to be taken together (compounding the effect of the medicine) so that we can recover faster. Given to us by the COMPOUNDER.

I never really ever gave this a thought as to why this person was called a compounder, its only now when I started writing this book that this clarity emerged.

In this superfast paced life, we fail to notice how Compounding touches us in so many ways and we don't even realize it. Let's see a few examples in real life of compounding.

Let's understand Compounding in the Money or Personal Finance Space, first!

CHAPTER *Four*

Compound Interest

Compound Interest

"If you understand Compound Interest You Basically Understand the Universe."

—Robert Breault

I have 100 Rs with me, I go to the Bank and tell them to keep it, in a bank account or a fixed deposit for 10 years and the Bank assures me an Interest Rate of 10%

Which means the bank will give me 10 Rs every year, year on year, for the next 10 years for the 100 Rs I've given them.

At the end of 10 years I get back my original 100, and the 10Rs I got every year which is 10 X 10= 100

Which means I get a total of 200

Now let's do something "Interesting"

I tell the bank instead of giving me the 10 every year, please Reinvest it back in the original 100. Which means at the end of year 1, I get 10, which I do not take but add it back to the 100, Now my balance with the bank becomes 110, at the end of year 1.

The next year, I'll get 10% on 110 which is 11, which means that at the end of the 2nd year my total amount with the bank is 121.

At the end of year 3, I get 10% on 121, which is 12.10 and this now gets added to the 121 which is already there with the bank and now my balance is 132.10

This now keeps happening every year for 10 years, the period I had selected to keep money in my Bank, Now, at the end of 10 years instead of 200, which I would have received if I wouldn't have reinvested the Interest, I have 259!

Let's do something a little more Interesting!

The bank is Paying me 10% yearly ie Rs 10 for every 100 kept with it, at the end of the year,

I go to the Bank and tell them instead of giving me 10 at the end of the year, give me 5, Half Yearly or every six months, and to reinvest this back in the original 100. Let's see how this Benefits Us.

So, at the end of six months 1 have 105, at the end of 1 year I have 110.25

At the end of 2 years I have 121.55 and so on, see the amounts are slowly but surely adding up. Compounding is working its magic!

This now keeps happening every six months for 10 years.

By doing this the maturity amount after 10 years becomes 265 instead of 259!

Let's expand this further to make it a little more interesting, let's ask the bank instead of paying us 5 every six months, to pay us 2.5 Rs every quarter and keep on reinvesting it till maturity.

If we do this, the final amount becomes 269!

This is how compounding works!

NO WONDER COMPOUNDING IS THE 8th WONDER

COMPOUNDING IS POWERFUL, COMPOUNDING NEEDS TIME!

Let me ask you another question and warn you in advance, most people, whom I have asked this question, have got the answer, wrong!

With the quarterly compounding after 10 years, my original 100 becomes 269,

What would happen if I do this for 20 years?

Please think and reply, do not use a calculator for answering this!

Most people say if in 10 years its 269 in 20 year it will double to 538!

WRONG!

That's not how compounding works!

AT the end of 20 years it does not double, it becomes 720, yes 720

Now go ahead use a calculator if you want and check it out!

The **human brain thinks in a linear way** which means that if we were asked to estimate what 10.22% compounded over 100 years would be then our answer is likely to be closer to 1,022% than 1,679,600%, something economists call *exponential growth bias*. This means that compounding *is often underestimated and should be at the heart of long-term investing."* Marathon Asset Management

This Table illustrates the how Compounding works in what we've discussed

Year	No Compounding	Yearly Compounding	Half Yearly Compounding	Quarterly Compounding
1	110	110	110.25	110.38
2	120	121	121.55	121.84
3	130	133.10	134.01	134.49
4	140	146.41	147.75	148.45
5	150	161.05	162.89	163.86
6	160	177.16	179.59	180.87
7	170	194.87	197.99	199.65
8	180	214.36	218.29	220.38
9	190	235.79	240.66	243.25
10	200	259.37	265.33	268.51
20	300	672.75	704	720.96
30	400	1744.94	1867.92	1935.81

This is what compounding does to your investments, the longer you stay invested, higher are the returns!

COMPOUNDING IS POWERFUL, COMPOUNDING TAKES TIME

Let's take another example in the Personal Finance space,

This is based on a real-life case that has happened with me, in the 50+ years of my family having been in Financial Services.

Twin brothers Ram and Shyam both after post-graduation start a job of a similar profile, at age 25.

Ram saves 10,000 every month for 10 years from age 25 to 35 then stops adding any new money to his savings. He doesn't withdraw anything and allows his investments to keep growing, to benefit from the power of compounding!

Shyam on the other hand wants to enjoy the good life, he spends his money on gadgets, like the latest model of iPhone, the latest SUV, goes partying on weekends with friends at 5 star hotels, eating out and buying expensive branded items like watches, goggles, sometimes to impress his, friends colleagues, sometimes to satisfy his ego. He wants to live the good life, He believes we only live once, it's important to live life King Size.

One day his brother Ram, Introduces Sham to the Financial Planner who had advised Ram about starting Investing early to benefit from the power of Compounding.

Shyam now, on the advice of this Financial Planner who shows him the results of his Twin brother Ram following his advice and consequently his investment portfolio having grown, agrees to start making Investments for his financial goals in life.

He also understands that he is late to start, so he agrees to start investing 20,000 every month from age 35 to 45.

Assuming the same 10% rate of return on both their savings, what do you feel will be the value of their investments at age 50?

Ram invested a total of 12,00,000 (10,000 X 12months X 10 years)

Shyam invested a total of 24,00,000 (20,000 X 12 months X 10 years)

At age 50 Ram has 83,48,811 and Shyam has 64,37,655!

Now look at this,

Ram has invested 12,00,000 only

Shyam has invested DOUBLE 24,00,000!

But Ram has made more money than Sham, How?

10000 every month for 10 years @ 10% becomes 1998638/-

That full amount then compounds to 8348811/- after 15 years @10% without adding any more money.

Shyam's investment of 20000 every month for 10 years @10% grew to 3997277 and then no more money was added, this amount in the next 5 years when Shyam reached age 50 grew @10% to 6437655/-

Ram gave his investments more time!

The power of compounding has worked to his advantage!

Even though Shyam invested DOUBLE of what Ram did he still made less money compared to Ram!

That's how Compounding works!

The more time you give to compounding the more powerful is its effect.

COMPOUNDING IS THE 8TH WONDER.
COMPOUNDING IS POWERFUL,
COMPOUNDING TAKES TIME.

CHAPTER Five

*Compound Interest
The Story Continues*

> *"The time to save for the future is now,*
> *Thanks to Compounding, the earlier you start putting money away for the future, the more will you make."*
>
> —*Alexa Von Tabel*

The Twin brothers, Ram and Sham got Married to Twin Sisters, Seeta and Geeta.

Both these couples were blessed with a child each, 2 years after they got married.

Seeta and Geeta both had a habit of keeping some money aside from the monthly budget for a rainy day, we know this, we've seen our Mothers, even our Grandmothers doing this when we were growing up.

Both the sisters consulted the same Financial Planner to take his advice on how to invest this money they had saved, at the time of the birth of their children, for their child's future like higher education or Marriage.

Seeta on the advice of their Planner, invested a single lumpsum of Rs 5,00,000 in a mutual fund scheme where she stayed invested till the child was 21 years old.

Geeta however was a little risk averse by nature and instead she decided to invest the same amount of 5,00,000 in a fixed deposit with a bank which guaranteed 7.5% for 21 years, because she was afraid of investing in Mutual

Compounding: The 8th Wonder

Funds! She always remembered disclaimer in Mutual Fund Advertisements where it was said, "Mutual Fund Investments are subject to Market Risks"!

When both their children reached the age of 21, Seeta's investment in the Mutual Fund grew at a RATE of 15% which resulted in a maturity amount of 94,10,759

(Ninety-Four Lakh Ten Thousand Seven Hundred Fifty-Nine)

Geeta's investment grew at an assured rate of 7.5%, exactly half as that of Seeta, but she managed to get ONLY 22,83,220/- (Twenty-Two Lakh, Eighty-Three Thousand Two Hundred and Twenty)

Now the rate of return of Geeta was exactly Half as that of Seeta, logically shouldn't she have made exactly half of what Seeta made, which is Forty-Seven lakh!

She made much lower! Twenty-two lakhs!

How?

Investment	Year	@7.5%	@15%
500000	1	537500	575000.00
	2	577812.50	661250.00
	3	621148.44	760437.50
	4	667734.57	874503.12
	5	717814.66	1005678.59
	6	771650.76	1156530.38
	7	829524.57	1330009.94
	8	891738.91	1529511.43
	9	958619.33	1758938.15

Investment	Year	@7.5%	@15%
	10	1030515.78	2022778.87
	11	1107804.46	2326195.70
	12	1190889.80	2675125.05
	13	1280206.53	3076393.81
	14	1376222.02	353852.88
	15	1479438.68	4068530.81
	16	1590396.58	4678810.44
	17	1709676.32	5380632.00
	18	1837902.04	6187726.80
	19	1975744.70	7115885.82
	20	2123925.55	8183268.70
	21	**2283219.97**	**9410759.00**

That's how compounding works!

There's 2 parts to Compounding, one and the most important part is time, how long do you give to your investments and the other, the rate at which it compounds!

For compounding to work for you, you have to give it time, longer the time better is the result.

COMPOUNDING IS THE 8th WONDER

COMPOUNDING IS POWERFUL.

COMPOUNDING TAKES TIME

REGULAR INVESTING, SIP/RD

There is no easier way to empower yourself than to repeat what works.

46 Compounding: The 8th Wonder

Repeat what works and see the effect of the Power of Compounding.

A very popular way of Saving money for the future to create a corpus is, the Monthly Recurring Deposit or the SIP (Systematic Investment Plan) wherein one can invest small amounts, regularly!

One can decide to invest a fixed amount Monthly, Quarterly, Half Yearly any frequency maybe even daily!

Let's see how a Monthly saving of 10,000 behaves at different rates of Interest over different Periods of time

The Table below shows how compounding works for different time lines.

MONTHLY DEPOSIT 10,000

Rate of Return	15 Years	20 Years	25 Years
6%	28,69,119	45,34,386	67,62,889
8%	3376063	56,89,990	90,89,909
10%	39,84,439	71,82,592	1,23,33,249
12%	47,14,578	91,12,110	1,68,62,065
14%	55,90,692	1,16,07,306	2,31,91,783
16%	66,41,566	1,48,33,712	3,20,40,017
18%	79,01,359	1,90,03,612	4,44,02,877

This one is an illustration of returns for Monthly or Systematic Investments, as you can see with regular investments, given time the amount invested, compounds to create a big corpus.

How does Compounding affect a single, lumpsum investment. Let's have a look what happens if one invests say 1,00,000/- one time,

What would be the result in different scenarios, rate and timewise,

Rate of Return	15 years	20 years	25 Years
6%	239655	320713	429187
8%	317216	466095	684847
10%	417724	672749	1083470
12%	547356	964629	1700006
14%	713793	1374348	2646191
15%	**813706**	**1636653**	**3291895**

I want you to notice the last row carefully, is there something that strikes you about the numbers?

The amount is DOUBLING, every five years

At a compounding rate of around 15% Money Doubles every 5 years.

In my Practice of 35 years in Financial Services, and now as a Financial Planner, this is the question I get asked most commonly by investors, both educated and not so educated types, the rich and not so rich, almost everyone. Tell me an investment that will DOUBLE my money!

IN how many years I ask them?

I don't know just tell me how to double my money!

My dear when do you want to double it?

That's not important just tell me a scheme where I can double my money!

I ask, how about Linking your Investment to a Financial Goal, like your child's higher education which is 7 or 8 or 10 years away, or your Silver Jubilee Wedding anniversary in 12 years away so that you can go for an International Holiday with your spouse, or something like that?

Normally I do not get an answer.

People are interested in DOUBLING Their money, most do not know when or how!

This Brings us to a very important Rule to Understand in COMPOUNDING, THE RULE OF 72.

CHAPTER Six

Compounding Rules

THE RULE OF 72

The Rule of 72 is useful in determining how fast money will grow.

If we know the annual rate of return in which an investment doubles, then if 72 is divided by that number, the answer we get is the number of years in which the investment will double.

Rule of 72

Investment Rate × Number of Years Invested = 72

Rule of 72

$$\text{Number of Years Invested} = \frac{72}{\text{Annual Investment Rate}}$$

Rule of 72

$$\text{Investment Rate} = \frac{72}{\text{Number of Years Invested}}$$

Let apply it.

An investment promises 7.2% rate of return, when will it double?

$$72/7.2$$

The answer is 10, It will take 10 years for an investment to double if the rate of return is 7.2%.

Let's take another one

The rate of return in an investment is 6%, when will it double

Applying the rule of 72

$$72/6$$

Answer is 12, The investment will double in 12 years!

There another way to look at the Rule of 72

If we know the number of years in which an Investment Doubles, then if we divide 72 by that number, the answer we get is the Annual Rate of Return

Let's understand by looking at a few examples

Around 25-30 years ago there used to be a very popular investment scheme in the Post Office called INDIRA VIKAS PATRA

Initially when it was launched it used to double the Investment in 5 years!

Yes, you read it right an assured return scheme by the Government of India, Doubling your money in 5 years

Let's use the Rule of 72 on that

$$72/5$$

The answer is 14.4, which means that your investment is compounding at the rate of 14.4% every year, or the interest rate is 14.4%

Remember the last table in the previous chapter we saw the money was doubling every 5 years if the Rate was 15%.

There was another Scheme in those days 20-25 years ago in the Post Office again, called NSC or the National Savings Certificate where the money used to double in 6 years. Let's apply the rule of 72 to this investment.

$$72/6$$

The answer is 12, which means that the rate of compounding or the interest rate was 12%

Another scheme called KISAN VIKAS PATRA which was launched many years ago and depending on the Rate at which it was offered there were times when the Investment doubled in 7 years, sometimes in 8 years and Nine years too.

Let's apply the Rule of 72

If it doubled in 8 years 72/8=9

The rate of return was 9%

In the case where it doubled in 9 years then 72/9=8 the rate of return was 8%

Annual Growth Rate	Years to Double	Annual Growth Rate	Years to Double
1%	72.0	11%	6.5
2%	36.0	12%	6.0
3%	24.0	13%	5.5
4%	18.0	14%	5.1
5%	14.4	15%	4.8
6%	12.0	16%	4.5
7%	10.3	17%	4.2
8%	9.0	18%	4.0
9%	8.0	19%	3.8
10%	7.2	20%	3.6

54 *Compounding: The 8th Wonder*

There are 2 more rules similar to the rule of 72, they are,

1. THE RULE OF 144

144 is a hint its double of 72

$$\frac{144}{\text{Rate of Return (\%)}} = \text{Time for investment to quadruple}$$

Time for investment to quadruple

The rule of 144 says that if you know the rate of return in an investment then if you divide 144 by that number the answer you get will tell you in how many years your investment QUADRUPLES

Or

If you know in how many years your investment QUADRUPLES, if you divide 144 by that number the answer tells you the Rate of return.

Let's look at a few examples.

An investment assures you 10% rate of return in how many years will it Quadruple?

Let's apply the Rule of 144

144/10 Answer is 14.4, Your investment will double in 14.4 years

Let's take another example

Your investment QUADRUPLES in 12 years what is the Rate of Return?

144/12 answer is 12

If an investment gives you 12% returns year on year every year then in 12 years this investment will QUADRUPLE!

2. The Rule of 114

Similar to the rules of 72 and 144, The RULE of 114 says that if you know the rate of return then if you divide 144 by that number then the answer you get is the number of years in which your money TRIPLES

Or

If you know in how many year's your money Triples, then if you divide 114 by that number the answer is your rate of return

$$\frac{144}{\text{Rate of Return (\%)}} = \text{Time for investment to triple}$$

Let's see a few examples.

Your money triples in 12 years what's the rate of return

114/12

Answer is 9.5

Your money will TRIPLE in 9.5 years if it compounds at the rate of 12%

Another

MY money grows at the rate of 10%, when will it Triple?

114/10

Answer is It will triple in 11.4 Years

In all the above examples in the tables and in all the above calculations the assumption of Compounding is YEARLY, this has been done to make it simple to understand.

CHAPTER Seven

CAGR - Compounded Annual Growth Rate

All the examples and illustrations we have seen up till now, there's one single assumption, that the rate of return on our investments is a constant, which means any investment grows at a fixed rate 6% or 8% or 10% every year, year on year till maturity.

Like in the Bank example we assumed a return of 10% for all the 10 years

The tables in the previous chapters assumed rates from 6% to 18% fixed over periods of 15-20-25 years

It is almost impossible to find an investment which can assure a fixed return over such long Periods.

Expecting Fixed returns over extended periods of time is not practical.

We saw that 25 years ago Indira Vikas Patra was offering 15% rate of return

The Rates on NSC and KVP have varied from 12% a few decades ago to somewhere around 7.3-7.5% currently, these change every quarter.

There was a time not so long ago when The Government of India Tax Free Bonds were giving assured 9% Tax Free Returns, those have slowly dropped. Now the Government does not issue these bonds at all!

If one wants to invest in these bonds it has to be bought from the Secondary Markets where the yield has fallen to 5.6%

It's impossible to assume that a fixed Rate of Return can be assured by any Bank, Institution or even a government over extended periods of time.

Worldwide in developed markets negative rates of return are a reality, which means if I keep money in the bank for one year and the rate is -2% at the end of one year I will get only 98.

We will discuss about this and negative compounding in later chapters.

I want to introduce you to a term called CAGR

COMPOUNDED ANNUAL GROWTH RATE.

We've seen a fixed rate of growth and what will the final amount grow to at that fixed rate of growth.

What if the growth rate was not assured, but a variable?

What if the money grew in some years and in some years, it didn't?

What if the money grew in some years and in some years it actually de grew, ie value went down!

What if it did nothing for long periods but in a few years, it gave outsized returns.

Are there investments like what I'm mentioning above?

How does your investment behave in such conditions, how is your behavior in those conditions?

That is what will finally determine the outcome, the amount of corpus that will get created from your investments.

CAGR - Compounded Annual Growth Rate

Let's start with a real-life example,

The year is 1979, and you have 100 rupees to invest in a new investment that has been launched.

Invest Rs 100 in this scheme, but there's no assurance of the rate of return, you will get in this scheme.

It will mature after 40 years. Because there's no assured Rate of return, there's no way of knowing how much will be returned to you after 40 years?

It is possible that the investment may grow, may fall, may do nothing, or may even go to zero!

How many of us will even consider this as an investment, something that doesn't assure a rate of return, something that doesn't assure you the capital that you've invested, something that's going to be locked in for the next 40 years, why would anyone invest in such a scheme, where there's no guarantee, no assurance?

After all when we invest money in an FD of a Bank or a Small Savings scheme of the Post Office there's a Certificate which we get which mentions the Rate of Return we will get on our Investment, the period of the investment and the date on which this investment will mature, with the maturity amount mentioned!

Now there were a select few investors, who decided even though, this investment is not assured, its risky, its volatile, let's give it a try!

By the way anyone could have invested any amount in this scheme, 100 is just the baseline, you could have invested, 100,200,500, 10,000, 100,000 or any amount of your choice.

Let's see what happened to those who were brave enough, did not look for assured returns and decided to take some risk and decided to invest.

40 years later all those who invested 100 have got 40,000!

Yes 40,000 with no assured Rate of Return, no assurance on the capital invested, a lot of risk with Volatility.

What scheme was this?

A few of you may have guessed it!

The BSE SENSEX it is!

THE BSE SENSEX was established in the year 1979, it became operational a few years later but it was rebased to 100 in 1979.

If someone had invested in the index and just stayed invested for 40 years that person would have received 40,000 this day, which translates to a return of 16.16% CAGR

Below figure shows the price movement of the initial 100 rupees invested till today.

CAGR - Compounded Annual Growth Rate

THE BSE SENSEX CHART since inception

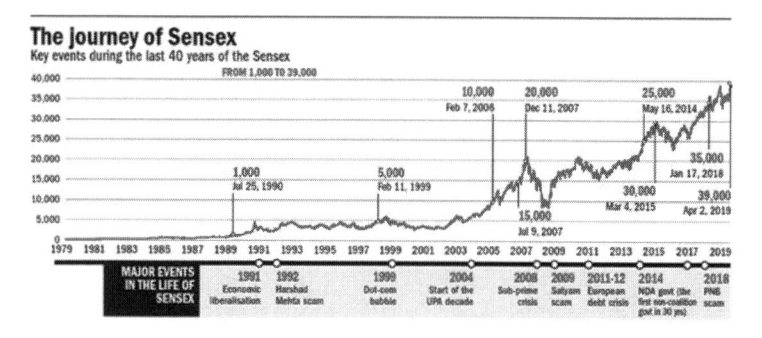

The Journey of Sensex
Key events during the last 40 years of the Sensex

Sensex Historical Yearly Returns - Since 1979

Sensex started at 100 in 1979 and has given below mentioned returns since then. It just shows how a volatile asset class who's return is not assured but if one stays invested for the long term, can compound the value of even a small investment of Rs 100 to 40,000. If you had more money to invest and let's say someone Invested 100000 in 1979 he would be sitting on a goldmine worth 4 crore today

Date	Sensex	1 Year Return
1979	100	
1980	129	28.57%
1981	173	34.90%
1982	218	25.52%
1983	212	-2.85%
1984	245	15.99%
1985	354	44.24%
1986	574	62.24%

Date	Sensex	1 Year Return
1987	510	-11.10%
1988	398	-21.94%
1989	714	79.13%
1990	781	9.45%
1991	1,168	49.54%
1992	4,285	266.88%
1993	2,281	-46.78%
1994	3,779	65.71%
1995	3,261	-13.71%
1996	3,367	3.24%
1997	3,361	-0.17%
1998	3,893	15.82%
1999	3,740	-3.92%
2000	5,001	33.73%
2001	3,604	-27.93%
2002	3,469	-3.75%
2003	3,049	-12.12%
2004	5,591	83.38%
2005	6,493	16.14%
2006	11,280	73.73%
2007	13,073	15.89%
2008	15,644	19.68%
2009	9,709	-37.94%
2010	17,528	80.54%
2011	19,445	10.94%
2012	17,404	-10.49%
2013	18836	8%

CAGR - Compounded Annual Growth Rate

Date	Sensex	1 Year Return
2014	22386	19%
2015	27957	25%
2016	25342	-9%
2017	29621	17%
2018	32969	11%

I've mentioned CAGR, which is COMPOUNDED ANNUAL GROWTH RATE,

How is this different form the rate of interest or rate of return which was mentioned many times ago?

As we see in the table, this investment has NEVER given returns in a straight line, it has been volatile, there have been years of negative returns, a year of ZERO returns, some years of superlative returns, never a fixed return for all the 40 years.

Thus the 16.16% is the value which is the average of the number of years one stayed invested.

Even though the returns have NOT Been in a straight line, there are clear and visible returns, which are the result of Compounding of the initial investment which was held on for this long period of 40 years

There are many who argue, wrongly, that equity as an asset class and consequently equity mutual funds should not be used as an example for the power of compounding. They say that Compounding works only when there are straight line assured returns.

66 *Compounding: The 8th Wonder*

I leave this open to you the readers, to decide, if an investment of 100 has become 40000 in 40 years, has it compounded in value or not?

Shouldn't this be a good example of the power of compounding

COMPOUNDING IS POWERFUL, COMPOUNDING TAKES TIME

We saw how the SENSEX which is composed of 30 stocks, has behaved over the course of 40 years/

Let's see how a few select stocks in and outside the Sensex have behaved over a period of time.

Company	From	To	Amount	Value	Years	CAGR
Infosys	Jun 1993	Oct 2017	10,000	29,730,645	24	**39%**
Eicher Motors	Jan 1990	Oct 2017	10,000	20,179,688	27.5	**32%**
HDFC Bank	May 1995	Oct 2017	10,000	2,246,957	22.5	**27%**
Asian Paints	Jan 1998	Oct 2017	10,000	5,90,3,500	30	**24%**

Let's see the actual price movement, it's not a straight line!

Infosys

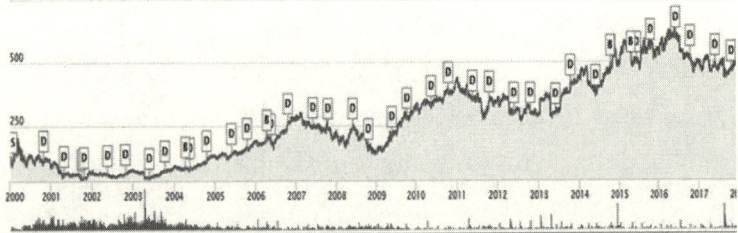

HDFC Bank

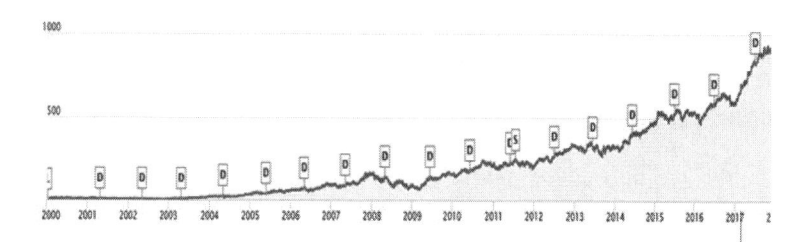

Eicher Motors

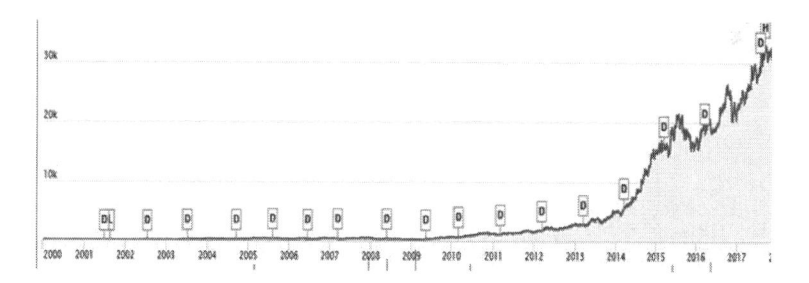

Asian Paints

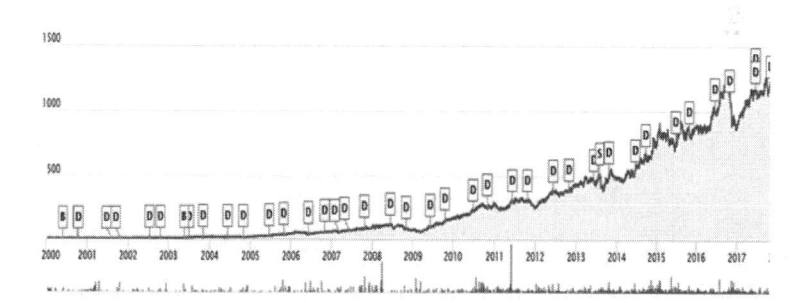

None of these charts show that the returns have been linear, however for those who stayed invested the returns are nothing short of spectacular! The most important thing seen here is the longer one has stayed invested the higher have been the returns!

THIS IS THE POWER OF COMPOUNDING. COMPOUNDING TAKES TIME.

In fact any investment one does in any asset class, be it equity, be it debt, be it commodities like Oil, be it Real Estate, be it Precious metals like Gold, Silver or Platinum or the newest craze in the last few years, BITCOIN, prices of all of them are volatile to say the least.

None of them promises any fixed returns, Prices are volatile but all of them have over the period of many years by the Power of Compounding, rewarded their Investors handsomely.

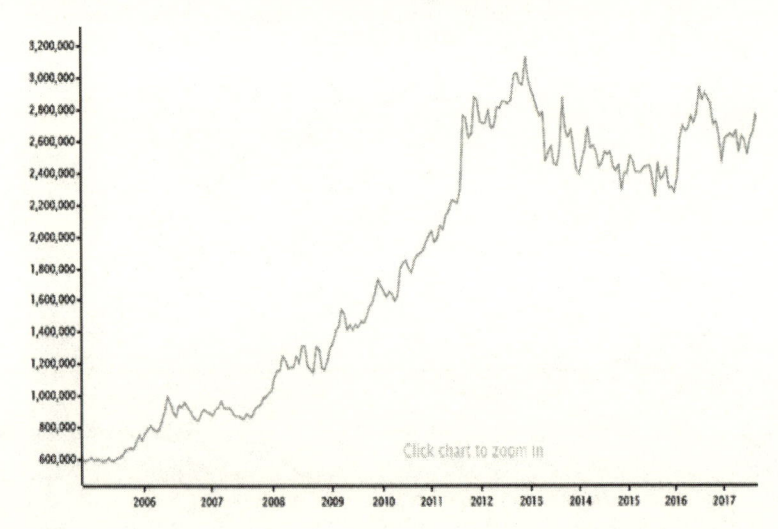

Gold Price Movement

CAGR - Compounded Annual Growth Rate

Bitcoin

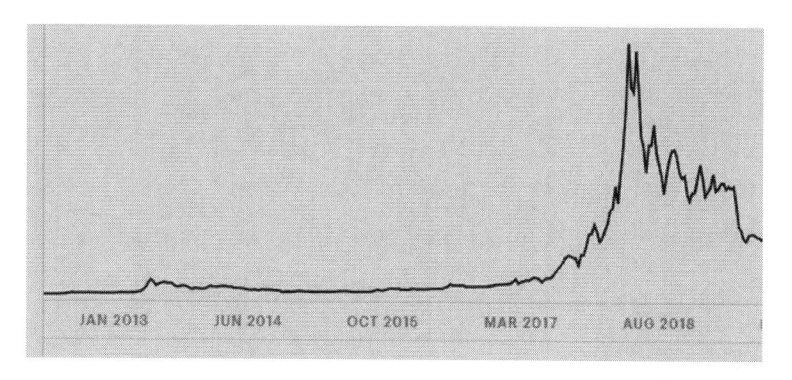

All asset classes by nature go through cycles of demand and supply, shortage and overproduction, affecting their prices, as a result affecting returns to investors who may have invested in them at different points of time during the asset cycle, however over the long period returns in most asset classes revert to the mean.

Warren Buffett is a legend; he is the most well-known and the richest investor in the world today!

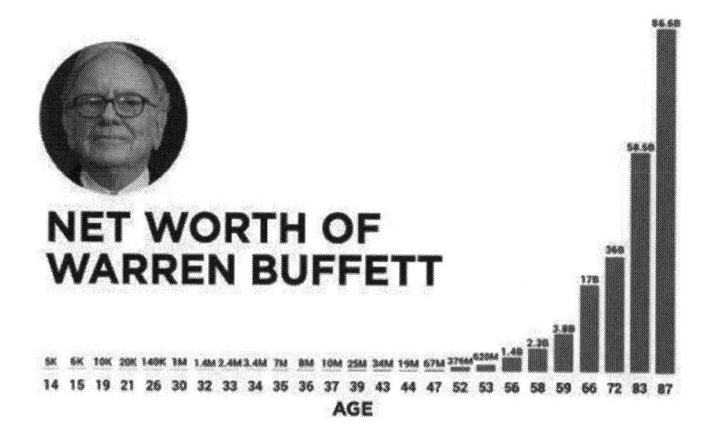

NET WORTH OF WARREN BUFFETT

Just look at how his net worth has moved.

The worth of warren Buffet, is it Linear, has it not compounded?

He started investing at an early age and kept on investing whenever he found an opportunity,

Buffett bought his first stock at 11, but has earned 99 percent of his wealth since his 50th birthday!

The Effect of Compounding

> COMPOUNDING IS THE 8th WONDER
> COMPOUNDING IS POWERFUL,
> COMPOUNDING TAKES TIME.

Famous quotes of Warren Buffett on Compounding

Successful Investing takes time, discipline and patience. No matter how great the talent or effort, some things just take time.

You only have to do a very few things right in your life so long as you don't do too many things wrong.

Compounding works not only in the money space but in all areas of Life as well.

In his book, *The One Thing: GARY KELLER says*

When you see someone who has a lot of knowledge, they learned it over time.
When you see someone who has a lot of skills, they developed them over time.

CAGR - Compounded Annual Growth Rate

*When you see someone who has done a lot,
they accomplished it over time.
When you see someone who has a lot of money,
they earned it over time.*

What is common in all of the above sentences TIME

COMPOUNDING is a result of giving TIME to whatever you do consistently!

COMPOUNDING IS POWERFUL COMPOUNDING TAKES TIME

CHAPTER Eight

The 10,000 Hours

10,000 HOURS

In his book *Outliers: The Story of Success*, Malcolm Gladwell mentions the "10,000-Hour Rule", claiming that the key to achieving world-class expertise in any skill, is, to a large extent, a matter of practicing the correct way, for a total of around 10,000 hours!

He says that the most successful people of the world, including sportsmen, business people, musicians and scientists, don't necessarily have a high IQ, that is not a basic requirement to succeed, but the key thing required is persistent, hard work, of around 10,000 hours.

Gladwell claims that greatness requires enormous time, He gives the example of the Beatles.

The Beatles started their career in the early 1960s, but theirs was not an overnight success. The Beatles' early on in their career would perform near military bases in Hamburg, Germany, **for eight hours a day, seven days a week.** They did this for 270 days over the course of 18 months.

By the time the Beatles enjoyed their first commercial success in 1964, **they had performed 1,200 times, which is more than most bands today perform in their careers.** They were well and truly on their way to getting in their 10,000 hours. Gladwell asserts that all of the time the Beatles spent performing, it shaped their talent, and by the time they returned to England from Hamburg, Germany, 'they sounded like no one else. It was the making of them.

Gladwell interviewed Microsoft co-founder Bill Gates to find out how he achieved his extreme wealth, he concludes that Gates met the 10,000-Hour Rule. Gates had the good fortune to attend a private school in Seattle that had a computer club. This was 1968, when most universities did not have a computer club. And Gates' club didn't have an ordinary computer — they had an ASR-33 Teletype, one of the most advanced computers available then. Gates spent his time on computers and began programming in the eighth grade and by the time he graduated, **Gates had practically lived in the computer lab for five years.** He was closing in on his 10,000 hours.

Gladwell explains that reaching the 10,000-Hour Rule, which he considers the key to success in any field, is simply a matter of practicing a specific task that can be accomplished with 20 hours of work a week for 10 years.

Ramit Sethi, the **New York Times** *best-selling author of the book,* **I Will Teach You to Be Rich**

In a guest post for INC.com writes,

Why Successful People Take 10 Years to 'Succeed Overnight'

He says There's a reason this 10-years-to-overnight-success pattern shows up over and over. And it's not just about working hard over a long period of time.

He says there's a deeper strategy used by successful people to level up that almost no one talks about called the Power of Sequence which is highly underappreciated.

The strategy that works over and over for successful people is the Domino Strategy.

The Domino Strategy is simple

First, start so small that you can easily knock over the first domino

Second, put the dominoes in just the right sequence so that each small step makes the next, bigger step possible.

With just 13 dominoes, a YouTuber created a two billion times amplification in energy. The first domino is just 5mm high. The largest domino weighs 100 pounds and is more than a meter tall. *With 16 more dominoes, there would be enough force to knock over the Empire State Building.*

You can watch the video here

https://www.youtube.com/watch?v=5JCm5FY-dEY

He goes on to give the example of Elon Musk, He says and I quote,

Most people have only heard of Musk in the past few years. To many, he seems like an overnight success. However, Musk has been focused on his vision since he was a teenager, and he's been consciously levelling up *for decades*

Throughout his teenage years, he read two books per day, more than a decade before he started Tesla, Musk was studying physics at the University of Pennsylvania and then battery technology at Stanford, both key fields for learning how to build an electric car

Warren Buffet who has already been mentioned in this book, before, says

By the age of 10, I'd read every book in the Omaha public library about investing, some twice!

You have to jump in the water, you'll soon find out whether you like it. The earlier you start, the better."

One of my Mentors SAM CAWTHORN, world famous Speaker, best - selling Author and Futurist from Australia says this repeatedly,

"If you are faithful to the small the big will come"

Jack Canfield, World famous best-selling author says,
"NO one becomes Successful Overnight, success is a

combination of hard work and opportunity, so keep working hard even when nobody is watching. One day You'll thank Yourself"

This is what repetition of doing small things, slowly becoming bigger and better does!

This is what compounding is, this is what compounding does!

COMPOUNDING IS POWERFUL, COMPOUNDING TAKES TIME.

NO WONDER COMPOUNDING IS THE 8TH WONDER OF THE WORLD.

Let's say an athlete wants to become the best at what he's doing, Running.

Can he win the Olympics Gold when he runs his first race? No way! It takes years and years of Practice just to qualify to get into your national team. Getting qualified to represent your nation in the Olympics is another thing altogether. Then winning the Olympics race.

We now understand that putting 10,000 hours will take around 10 years. This means, if an athlete wants to become an Olympian at 21, they need to have started when they were 10-12 years old! You would have to give 10 years of your prime, to doing only one thing, running in this case to continuously becoming better at what you do.

To win at the Olympics you may have to put in another 3000-5000 hours of hard gruelling practice!

"Nothing can substitute for just plain hard work... If you don't practice, you don't deserve to win" (Andre Agassi)

The 10,000-hour rule doesn't just apply to performers and professional athletes. Businessmen or scientists, it also applies to any of us who wants to become an expert in our chosen profession.

Bruce Lee is quoted to having said

"I fear not the man who has practiced 10,000 different kicks, I fear the man who has practiced one kick 10,000 times."

He says if there's someone who's been practicing 10,000 different kicks, even though regularly, I have no problem, I know I can beat him, because even though he is giving time he is not being able to compound his actions.

If someone, however has practiced 1 kick 10,000 times, I would find it difficult to beat him as his actions have compounded, he's now an expert at doing that one thing.

Is there some magic in the 10,000 number? Does it mean it needs 10,000 hours and 9000 will not do or 8500, or any number for that matter NO! It just means you need to put in a lot of effort and hard work, maybe even smart work to become world-class in anything that you start out to become!

The important question now is, "What is that smart work?

A Taxi driver decides, I've been driving a car regularly and I have an experience of driving for 10,000 hours. I now am an expert and I will participate and win the Formula 1 championship! Can he win, No! he can participate for sure and maybe even get injured in the process, driving a taxi and a racing car are 2 completely different thing! He hasn't practiced in a race car, or driven a race car ever and driving a Taxi in the city is different from driving a formula 1 racing car.

However, the 10,000 hours rule is often misunderstood as **"any 10,000 hours"** spent on your skill or craft. But not all practice is the same: there's a big difference between mindless repetition and what scientists call deliberate practice.

"James Clear Author of the Best Seller "Atomic Habits" says there's something called."

—*Deliberate Practice*

Deliberate practice refers to a special type of practice that is **purposeful** and **systematic**. While regular practice might include mindless repetitions, deliberate practice requires focused attention and is conducted with the specific goal of improving performance.

Deliberate practice *does not* mean that you can fashion yourself into anything with enough work and effort, though. While human beings do possess a remarkable ability to develop their skills, there are limits to how far any individual can go.

Deliberate practice can help us maximize our potential. It turns potential into reality.

As you practice regularly, the synapses between the neural connections in your brain, strengthen, allowing information to pass between them more efficiently. They become myelinated. Myelin, is a component of white matter, which is a fatty tissue that insulates axons. Myelin helps move information across axons faster and with greater intensity.

The closer you get to your 10,000 hours of practice, the better and stronger are your neural connections.

Neurologist Daniel Levitin says, "It doesn't mean that if you put in 10,000 hours that you will become an expert, but there aren't any cases where someone has achieved world-class mastery without it." Time spent perfecting an activity, coupled with performing it correctly, is the most influential factor in becoming an expert at it

Expertise is a process, not an outcome, it happens, over Time.

COMPOUNDING IS POWERFUL,
COMPOUNDING TAKES TIME.

CHAPTER
Nine

Catalyst

The meaning of the word CATALYST at Dictionary. Com is

Something that causes activity between two or more persons or forces without itself being affected.

A person or thing that precipitates an event or change

A person whose talk, enthusiasm, or energy causes others to be more friendly, enthusiastic, or energetic.

In Chemistry. a substance that causes or accelerates a chemical reaction without itself being affected.

Let's see how a catalyst can help speed up the process of Compounding!

Brian Tracy, motivational public speaker and self-development author of over seventy books *says "No one lives long enough to learn everything they need to learn starting from scratch. To be successful, we absolutely, positively have to find people who have already paid the price to learn the things that we need to learn to achieve our goals."*

Let's go the example of the Athlete who wants to become an Olympian and go on to win the gold medal. Let's say he has put in his 10,000 hours of practice, can he go on to win, does he really tick all the boxes when it comes to winning an Olympic Gold medals?

It takes so much more than only practice, nobody can succeed at anything in life without the support of those people around them, their family and friends, and for a sportsperson in any field, an athlete, in particular, can never win without having a coach, who acts as a catalyst!

Just add the number of hours and years a coach has put in to become who he is now, an expert who can help others, he's probably put in 20,0000 hours or more!

To get to the top, coaching is a huge factor in the development of an athlete. A Coach gives confidence and experiential knowledge which can be used by the trainee athlete to get to where he wants without actually putting in his 10,000 hours, he may actually need only 5000 hours of deliberate Practice which is fine tuned with the expertise of the coach.

This athlete now, has his 5000 hours of deliberate practice, plus the expertise of 20000 hours of his coach which actually means he's now having a compounded experience of 25000 hours of experiential practice! Put in the hours of support by friends and family on this journey and they've probably crossed 50,000 hours. There's no way this athlete will not win!

Ask any top athlete, A winner in any sport, whether it be at the Olympics or any professional event, they will always give the credit to their coach, first, for getting them there at the top.

Sachin Tendulkar, one of the greatest cricket batsmen of all time, says this about his Coach Ramakant Achrekar,

"My coach has built the foundation of my cricketing career; He did not just provide education but also values. He taught me to play straight - on the field and in life. I shall always remain grateful to him for his immeasurable contribution in my life. His lessons continue to guide me today".

Usain Bolt in response to the importance of his coach Glen Mills, says and I quote

"He has always made the right decisions for me. He is a guiding light in my career and he has shown me the way to improve myself both as a person and as an athlete,"

The first words the British swimmer Ellie Simmonds said after winning the gold medal in the Paralympics 400m freestyle event at London 2012, *"I am exhausted, I just can't wait to see my coach"*

Read the biographies of famous athletes, sportspersons, any professional, there's one thing they all agree upon, that success most certainly does not happen quickly. In fact, it takes many years of dedication and hard work to achieve the level of success, they have, and nothing would have been possible without their coach or their mentor who acted like a CATALYST for things to have not only happened but to have speeded up.

Atul Gawande, MD, MPH, the CEO of Haven, the Amazon, Berkshire Hathaway, JPMorgan Chase health care venture, and a globally recognized surgeon, writer, and public health leader has given a TED talk titled: ***Want to get great at something? Get a coach.***

He asks: How do I get better at what I do? How Do professionals get better at what they do? How do they get great?

There are two views about how professionals get great. One is through practice and their own improvement.

Second is "You are never done, everybody needs a coach, everyone"

He says he always believed that expertise was not needing a coach,

Gawande says he paid someone, a former retired professor of his, to observe his surgeries, comment on them and critique him as a coach.

The first time when he did a surgery with his coach in the surgery room, it went well and he was expecting his coach to have very little feedback. To his surprise his coach had pages of notes and little improvements that he could make in the operating room. Taking feedback from his Coach, working upon it, transformed Gawande from a good surgeon to a great one.

His Coach was a CATALYST in making him better, within 2 months he thought he was much better and within a year there was massive improvement.

He says Coaches are your external eyes and ears and they provide you with an accurate picture of your reality.

He sees the same opportunity for any professional looking to get better.

Add a catalyst and see how things in life compound, be it Health, Wealth, Relationships, anything and everything happens quicker, faster making you better!

Remember the example of Seeta and Geeta in one of the earlier chapters, Seeta made much higher than Geeta even though both invested the same amount for the same period, but Seeta followed her Planners advice, her Coach, Trusting his expertise, whereas Geeta was afraid of volatility and instead of following the advice of her CATALYST, the Planner, she decided to go the safer route.

The difference is stark!

If you recall both had invested 50000 each in an investment for 21 years, Seeta's grew at 15% and Geeta's grew at 7.5%

SEETA got 94,10,759

GEETA Got 22,83,2198

Geeta a few years later understands that she should have followed the advice of her Planner and invested her money, as per his recommendations.

So, after completing 10 years in her current investment strategy, she moves her money, which now has grown to 1030515/- to the investment plan suggested by her planner, she now has 11 years left till her child reaches 21.

That money is now expected to grow to 4794359/- at the end of 21 years, which is more than double of what she would have got if she stuck to her original plan!

No new money was added, the existing corpus was just shifted to a better investment by following the advice of a Planner, a CATALYST who created so much value.

The most Common New Year resolution is to Join the gym and to lose weight and get in shape!

Let's say you decide to go to the gym regularly on the advice of your doctor as you have put on weight. You join the Gym at the beginning of the new year and your resolution is to lose 10 Kgs in the next one year.

You start exercising on your own for the first few days and weeks. You see results initially but then it tapers off and Data shows that 80% of new year resolutions fail by Feb, the top being Joining a gym to lose weight and get in shape!

There will always be reasons to put off your daily gym visit due to some reason or another.

However, if you enlist the help of a Personal Trainer, someone who helps you, pushes you, advises you on the Right Exercise, Diet and puts you on a plan, chances are you'll achieve your results well ahead of time. The trainer didn't do the exercises, you did, the effort was put in by you, but the Trainer is your coach and acts like a catalyst, helping you in losing weight and becoming a fitter, healthier person, faster.

In Chemistry a catalyst helps a reaction to happen faster, without the catalyst getting affected and the reaction speeds up.

A few real-life examples of Catalysts we normally do not observe or appreciate,

The catalytic converter in a car contains platinum, which serves as a catalyst to convert carbon monoxide, which is highly toxic, into carbon dioxide., which is relatively safer.

Enzymes in our body and in foods are biology's natural catalysts. They play a role in digestion of food by helping break down food and helps in absorption of nutrients in our body.

Beer and Bread are typically made with yeast, a catalyst which is a living organism containing enzymes. When we use laundry detergents to get rid of stains on our clothing, it contains a catalyst in action during a chemical reaction. Detergents have enzymes, which help break up dirt and other stains on clothing.

Catalysts help break down paper pulp in Paper factories to produce the smooth paper we get to use in everyday life.

Catalysts help turn milk into yogurt and the Petroleum extracted from the earth is converted into many types of plastic, which we use in our lives in different forms every day.

CHAPTER
Ten

Habits Compound

> "We are what we repeatedly do, Excellence, then is not an act but a habit."
>
> —Aristotle

James Clear writes in his Book Atomic Habits:

Habits are the compound interest of self-improvement. The same way that money multiplies through compound interest, the effects of your habits multiply as you repeat them. They seem to make little difference on any given day and yet the impact they deliver over the months and years can be enormous. It is only when looking back two, five, or perhaps ten years later that the value of good habits and the cost of bad ones becomes strikingly apparent.

There's this story of a world-Famous Surgeon who had done 400+ Heart Surgeries and his Surgeries were 100% Successful. Not a single patient of his, had died, during surgery, EVER!

Due to this unique achievement of his, he was in great demand especially amongst celebrities and VIPs who were ready to pay him any amount as Professional Fees, as they had the comfort of knowing his track record of no one having died during surgery.

He also had a habit of spending the night, before the Planned Surgery with his Patient on whom he was going to operate the next day.

During one such stay with a high-profile celebrity, he was reading a book about how to conduct a successful surgery, when the celebrity came and saw him reading this book!

He asked the Surgeon, you have performed more than 400 Successful Surgeries, why do you need to read a book about How to perform a Surgery?

He answered it's because I read this book, before each and every Surgery of mine, that I am able to perform a successful Surgery and that's how I have this record!

Abraham Lincoln, who was a skilled woodcutter before becoming one of the most important presidents in US history said: "If I had six hours to chop down a tree, I'd spend the first four hours *sharpening the axe*

If I had 8 hours to chop down a tree, I would spend 6 of those hours sharpening my axe.

Doing things repeatedly, regularly makes it a habit, which compounds!

I remember when we were growing up there was always this one message from my parents, to me and my 2 sisters,

Develop good habits when you are small, hang around with those kids in school who excel in studies, who are good in sports and stay away from those with bad habits!

it's our habits that ultimately decide what we do *and* who we become, according to researchers from Duke University, up to 40% of our behaviours on any given day are driven by habit.

An ancient story goes like this, Plato the great philosopher of his time saw a boy playing a gambling game with his friend not with money but nuts! He scolded the boy for doing so, the boy asked Plato, you are scolding me for such a small matter! Plato replied, Habit is not a small matter!

He understood the power of habits, the power of doing things repeatedly, the power of compounding

It's said HABITS MAKETH THE MAN

JIM ROHN, the mentor of Tony Robbins, one of the world's greatest Motivators, says this,

Motivation is what keeps you started; habits keep you going!

It is said what you do everyday matters more than what you do once in a while, Habit and Routine have Unbelievable power!

Quoting James Clear from his Book "Atomic Habits"

Habits are like the atoms of our lives. Each one is a fundamental unit that contributes to your overall improvement. At first, these tiny routines seem insignificant, but soon they build on each other and fuel bigger wins that multiply to a degree that far outweighs the cost of their

initial investment. They are both small and mighty. This is the meaning of the phrase atomic habits—a regular practice or routine that is not only small and easy to do, but also the source of incredible power; a component of the system of compound growth.

Habits that seem small and unimportant at first will compound into remarkable results if you're willing to stick with them for years. The big changes you want to make in your life (stopping smoking, getting in shape, becoming a better singer, better writer, better whatever) are just the culmination of thousands of tiny actions, **tiny little things, practiced regularly, add up to massive results.**

The power of habits is in their compounding ability. The more you keep them up, the bigger the return, **small actions done regularly, produce have massive results,**

Habits compound over Time.

If you Want more wealth, Invest money, Regularly

If you Want Better health, Exercise regularly

If you Want better Relationships, Give time to your loved ones, Regularly.

If you Want to get better at your craft, Practice it, Regularly

If you Want to become a writer, Read and write, Regularly

If you Want to achieve inner peace and Tranquillity, Practice Meditation, Regularly

Habits can be good; Habits can be bad!

If good habits compound, Bad Habits also Compound!

This brings us to the negative effects of compounding.

CHAPTER
Eleven

Negative Compounding

"Compounding *Is Not an Equal-Opportunity Mechanism. Its Rewards and Penalties Are Asymmetrical"* Frank Martin

We all now understand that habits compound, but if habits are bad, they too compound with a negative effect.

Smokers know that smoking causes cancer, smoking kills, every box of cigarettes comes with a pictorial warning, alongside a warning in text, but does a smoker stop smoking? No, why, It's a Habit, a bad habit! Does a smoker smoke more cigarettes than he or she was a few years, ago the answer is YES!

The power of negative compounding!

The same goes with any bad habit like, alcohol or drugs, that's why it's called an addiction, addiction is a result of the power of compounding.

Health is like a bank account with compounding interest. What you invest in your health on a daily basis, it compounds and grows over time.

Bad eating habits compound, if one keeps eating junk food not exercising not taking care of their health all these habits compound, if you never invest in your health and maintain high levels of stress, these habits also compound over time and deteriorate your quality of life.

However, when anyone decides to exercise for even45 minutes per day, they are investing in their own health with healthy habits, the results of which compound over time and shows on your physique, your skin, your attitude and your mind.

A great way to understand and appreciate the negative effect of compounding in the personal finance space is to miss a credit card outstanding bill by even one day! You will pay the interest on the full amount which was supposedly free when you spent it. Now you are forced to pay the interest till the next billing due date.

Another way credit cards issuers trick you is to allow you to make only a part payment of your outstanding bill by making a minimum payment.

Let's assume you made a minimum payment of 10% of the outstanding amount. You're under the impression that you have to pay the interest on the balance 90%.

NO

You have to pay the interest on the entire outstanding original amount even though you have made a 10% down payment, god forbid if you miss to pay the bill next month then you will be paying a compounded interest calculated on the outstanding for two months now and the interest rate on credit cards ranges in the range of 35-45 %

That's almost 3-35% interest rate per month. In some cards its compounded Daily!

Don't make the mistake of thinking that the minimum due is a "monthly payment" you should be making to pay off your credit card bill. When you only pay the minimum due on your credit card statement, your credit card issuer will make a lot of extra money from you

If you carry any of that balance into the next billing cycle, you'll be charged interest on it, *including the interest the credit card company added to your bill last month!*

This is "compounding of interest and charges" The bank charges interest on the entire balance outstanding, including any finance charges, every time interest is calculated. This is how credit card debt quickly snowballs into larger and larger amounts, making it difficult to come out of it.

Credit cards are designed to help the lenders, the issuing banks. Credit card monthly repayments are usually set so you are encouraged to keep borrowing and thus keep paying interest, and then interest on interest.

COMPOUNDIG IS POWERFUL only in this case for the lender not the borrower.

Another example of negative compounding is INFLATION

In the western world Governments and Central banks are trying to bring in inflation, however in developing countries inflation is a concern especially when you are planning for long term goals such as retirement

Let's say you are investing to create your nest egg, a corpus that will take care of your expenses when you are retired. Let's assume a 12% return over a regular investment of 25,000 per month for the next 20 years.

The future value or the corpus that will be created is 2,27,80,276/-

Now assume inflation of 5%, which means the cost of everything one consumes, goods and services are growing by 5% each year. Which means if this is factored in to the corpus value now the value reduces to 1,26,88,409/-

Inflation which is invisible has negatively impacted the value of the corpus you had started out to create, which also means that if you want to create an inflation adjusted corpus of 22780276, you will have to invest not 25,000 every month but 44884/-

COMPOUNDING IS POWERFUL AND COMPOUNDING TAKES TIME.

CHAPTER Twelve

Compounding in Nature

There's a saying

> "The greatest oak was once a little nut
> who held its ground."
>
> —Author Unknown

A healthy oak sapling takes 15 to 20 years to reach maturity, but it can take as many as 50 years before an oak will produce acorns. Planting an oak tree will make generations to come happy because of the thick shade it will provide them with. These trees can actually live for more than 200 years.

The "major oak" in Sherwood forest is thought to be 1,200 years old!

A tree living for 1200 years from the day it was Planted!

The Great Basin bristlecone pine, in the white mountains California USA is the oldest known living tree in the world? It is estimated to be 4851 years old!

How did this happen? COMPOUNDING

We all love to eat fruits, It's the most basic form of complete nutrition given to us by Nature.

In India the alphonso mango is referred to as the king of Fruits, we get torelish it at the beginning of Summer every year.

The Mango seed when planted, needs to be nurtured, given water, sunshine and fertilizer, for at least 5-7 years, before it can produce any fruit. For these first 5-7 years there's no Fruit, no output, nothing at all.

If I was a mango farmer, I would wonder why am I doing this at all, all work, no results.

However, once this fully-grown tree starts producing fruit, after the initial 5-7 years, it then keeps on giving us delicious alphonso mangoes, for years together, for life, till it is standing tall.

Once it has started producing fruit, then we do not need to bother about nurturing it, giving it water and fertilizer as the roots have entrenched so deep into the ground that it can take care of its needs. All it now does is produce delicious lip-smacking mangoes every year.

This is the effect of compounding, Compounding is Powerful, Compounding Takes Time.

Same is the case with a fruit that we have been introduced to recently.

Till a few years ago few of us had even heard about The Avocado.

The avocado seed after planting needs to be nourished and taken care of for 10-15 years for it to produce the first fruit. You read it right 10-15 years!

Once it does that that it keeps on producing fruit, almost forever.

Another example from nature is the Delicious Date popularly known is India as Khajoor

Dates have been a staple food of the Middle East and the Indus Valley for thousands of years.

Date palms can take 4 to 8 years after planting before they will bear fruit!

It is found in dry hot desert regions, but the nutritional value it provides is immense.

One can go with only eating dates and nothing else for days together in these areas.

But one the best example of the Power of compounding is the Chinese bamboo Tree!

Plant the Chinese bamboo seed and keep on giving it water and fertilizer and it does NOTHING for the first year,

It does nothing for the second year, nothing for the 3rd and the 4th year, It does nothing till 10 months of the 5th year,

It's just growing beneath the ground and getting ready to come out.

Now a miracle happens in the next 4-6 weeks, it grows 70-90 feet. Yes 70-90 feet

The Chinese bamboo tree has been recorded at growing upwards of 2.5-3 feet a day.

Now, just imagine, the farmer who had planted the seed and saw no growth in 4 years and 10 months had he stopped nurturing that seed, the seed would never have sprouted and grown into the tree.

That's compounding from nature, for you.

COMPOUNDING IS POWERFUL, COMPOUNDING TAKES TIME.

There are so many examples from nature in the fruit and tree section which are good examples of the powerful effect of compounding and the fact that compounding needs time

Fruit trees vary in the amount of time it takes a plant to grow to the time it produces its first fruits.

Sweet cherry trees and pawpaw trees are some of the slowest and can take up to seven years to yield a crop.

The peach tree takes between 2-4 years to fruit.

An apricot tree, An Apple Tree, takes 2-5 years to fruit.

The Plum Tree, The Pear Tree take 4-5 years to bear fruit.

CHAPTER Thirteen

The Rubiks Cube

The Rubiks Cube

The Rubik's Cube is toy which was invented in 1974 by Hungarian architecture and design professor Erno Rubik

We've all seen it at some time, in our lives when we were younger or every few years, when it becomes a rage amongst children and adults alike, many people have played around with this fascinating toy, and throughout the years there has been a number of competitions, challenges and variations for solving it.

The popularity of the Rubik's Cube can be attributed to the way it is designed, the six faces of the cube can be rotated freely, and the challenge is to bring it back to the original solved pattern of each side having the same colours after having shuffled it.

There are 18 basic moves that can be applied to a Rubik's Cube, rotating one of the six faces - front, back, up, down, left, or right, either 90° clockwise, 90° counter clockwise, or 180°

But it is mathematically complicated - there are 43 quintillion possible configurations of the Cube!

Using the power of extremely powerful supercomputers at Google, a group of mathematicians showed that that any cube could be solved in at most 20 moves.

Solving the cube is not easy for beginners, in fact it took the inventor Erno Rubik a month to solve it!

You need to keep at it, trying out different permutations and combinations before one can perfect the art of solving it.

Keep on taking small, regular steps till you get it right,

I remember the first time I tried solving it, It took me a few weeks and that too with help from someone who knew how to do it.

The world record for hand-solving by a human is 4.22 seconds!

4.22 seconds, can we even imagine that, could it have done it without having put in hours and hours of rigorous practice, trying out various permutations and combinations?

NO way.

It's a result of taking regular steps at trying to solve it and giving it a lot of time till the art of solving it in record time was perfected!

THE POWER OF COMPOUNDING, COMPOUNDING TAKES TIME!

CHAPTER Fourteen

Compounding in Education

Compounding in Education

It takes at least 21 years to be able to Graduate in any discipline after having attended school and college.

If we consider having spent 5 hours daily each day for 20 days every month, 10 months a year in 21 years we've given 21,000 hours to our studies in school and college

We start form Nursery, Kindergarten, Primary school years, Secondary school and finally College, starting with learning the Alphabet, in our very first class after which slowly but surely, we are introduced to newer subjects, newer languages, and so on.

After having given 21,000 hours of our prime one is able to stand up and get counted as a Graduate.

For many, education ends when they complete graduation, but, a select few take it upon themselves to learn more, by going on to becoming Professionals like Doctors, Lawyers, Chartered Accountants. They will now need to put at least another 10,000 hours to becoming an expert in their profession! the effect of their learning over time compounds.

To become good at anything we do, we have to give time. To Excel at something we have to give a lot more time. To become at Expert at that something, we have to still put in a lot more time.

Let me ask you 1 question, there's this ONE person in this world, that all of us know who has benefitted tremendously from the power of compounding, ONE PERSON.

Whenever I've asked this question, before, in a roomful of people, the answers I've commonly got are Warren Buffett, Charlie Munger, in the Indian Context people say Rakesh Jhunjhunwala, and some give other popular names.

But let's look at this, I told you sometime back that compounding isn't only about money. There's so much more to compounding!

YOU my dear READERS each and every one of you, reading this book, YOU are the biggest beneficiary of the Power of Compounding.

Remember you were born 7-8 pounds and now you are 90,100,120, maybe even 150 pounds! right! You personally, each one of you is the best example of the power of compounding.

Ever since you were born, till today, each and every day you have been given Food, Air, Water, you have given time to learning, gaining experience in your job or profession, you have given time to your health by eating well, exercising and a result of all that has compounded into what you are, today!

We all individually are the 8th Wonder of the world, we are unique, each one of us, there isn't anyone exactly like us, Isn't that a wonder?

CHAPTER Fifteen

Compounding in Life

There are many areas in our life where the actions we take can facilitate a compound effort over a larger period of time.

Here are just a few.

Compound Health – Eating healthy food, following a regular exercise routine, and taking care of your mental health, all will lead to compounding effects on your overall health. The daily are small, but over time one can improve their health exponentially

Compound Relationships – Putting efforts into creating new relationships, as well as nurturing existing ones, by giving time, can have a compound effect. Not only will have more meaningful relationships, but you'll also gain a better understanding of those around you.

Compound Knowledge – The more you seek to expand your knowledge, by continuous education, by learning new systems, skills and newer ways of thinking, new perspectives and opportunities keep opening up.

Compound Optimism – Optimism is a mindset that needs time to grow. As you begin to create a positive mindset, you'll find more opportunities and better outcomes in whatever you do in life!

How to Use Compounding

The key to compounding is **building a positive habit.**

Identify an area in your life that you want to grow, you can work backwards and think about what daily/weekly/monthly habits you can build to help you get there. Focusing on the short-term habits allows you to create small wins early on, and large wins over the really long term.

Not every activity will have a measurable success rate of return, over time. If you're doing something which you aren't really interested in, then even if you put in efforts and long hours, if your heart and mind isn't in it, there won't be any real results.

If you want to be run the marathon, become an accomplished singer or a musical instrument player, or an influencer in your community, you are going to need to continually invest a lot of effort over a long period of time. Building on success, and learning from failure will get you there.

The biggest benefits in life come from compounding. Relationships, habits, money, success, and growth are the result of making small investments in the right things and watching those investments grow (on top of each other) over time.

A few "investing" principles that are important to harness the power of compounding, which will lead to exponential growth.

Invest Regularly

The first thing is simply to invest regularly. Those who consistently make small deposits will reap the benefits of compounding over the course of time. Investing regularly allows your investments to grow on top of your investments—this applies to your health, wealth, people, and relationships.

Think about this concept for a sportsperson and his team. The coach invests in helping his players to become smarter, better skilled, and that initial investment by the coach does benefit that specific player, but that better player can with his performances lift up the entire team. That player is now more equipped to multiply the coach's influence throughout the group. The principle of multiplication is a powerful force. The more time, energy, and care that you invest in the lives of people around you, the stronger your team will become.

Invest for the long term.

Successful investors invest for the long term. When asked what is his investment horizon Warren Buffett replied FOREVER! Long Term investors are not bothered about volatility, in fact that is considered as an opportunity, when others are selling, they are buying and vice versa.

Big things happen by doing small things regularly that build up over time.

Compounding is accrued in money, life, health, relationships and leadership.

You don't build a strong body in a day, month, or even a year. It takes years of consistent effort. Shortcuts don't exist, no matter how 'smart' you work. If you eat an unhealthy meal, it won't give you a heart attack, tonight! But if you keep eating bad food every day for months and years, it will absolutely destroy your health.

If you want to see the impact of compounding in your own life, it requires you to focus on one thing at a time (for every aspect of your life) and always look at the bigger picture.

It applies to your health. Try running a marathon today. Unless you already are a marathon runner, you can't. But if you spend focused time and energy of practicing running, you will be able to run your first marathon maybe in 6 months. Your strength will compound. For the first few days and weeks you won't be able to run even a single mile. But by the end of the 6 months you will be running 26 miles, easily.

It comes down to this: You'll get there if you put in the work. Who cares if it's tomorrow or 20 years? It *will* happen. That's all that matters.

CHAPTER
Sixteen

Compounding in Language

Remember we had discussed earlier about the meaning of compound where 2 unique elements combine to form another, a similar thing happens a lot in our language, in any language for that matter.

Compound Words

Compound words are formed when two or more words are put together to form a new word with a new meaning.

Closed compound words are formed when two unique words are joined together. They don't have a space between them and they are the type that generally comes to mind when we think of compound words. For example:

Bookstore	Baseball
Fireworks	Grandmother
Airplane	Notebook

Open compound words have a space between the words but when they are read together a new meaning is formed:

Ice cream	Post office
Full moon	Dinner Table
Hot dog	Living room

Hyphenated compound as the name suggests are words connected by a hyphen

Daughter-in-law	Check-in
Eighty-six	One-third
Merry-go-round	Well-being

CHAPTER Seventeen

Fastest Compounding in The World!

I firmly believe this is the example of the fastest effect of compounding anywhere in nature.

How does a single cell become a person?

Immediately upon conception, the first cell splits to become two and the two becomes four and so on. After just 47 doublings, there are ten thousand trillion (10,000,000,000,000,000) cells in your body which have gone and arranged in such a fashion so as to produce, bones, muscles, skin, hair, different organs of the body like the brain, eyes, nose, mouth, stomach, intestines, liver, pancreas, and so on and each and everything required to create a human being, that too Within 9 months!

Understanding the importance of compounding in life can help one enjoy and live life to the fullest, very similar to how compounding helps grow one's investments over the years so as to help achieve life goals.

CHAPTER
Eighteen

Real Life Heroes Compounding

Before they tasted success, many of the world's now considered most successful people experienced epic failure, for years together.

AMITABH BACHHAN

"Perfection needs effort to get it right. I need to rehearse for it. Many others who are greatly more efficient than me, do not. To each his craft! And I am no legend!"

—*Amitabh Bachchan*

Amitabh Bachchan completed 50 years in Bollywood in November 2019. For me and many who grew up watching his films in the 70s and 80s he is truly the SHAHENSHAH of Bollywood.

He's visible everywhere, on TV, in Cinemas playing a part or in Ads, promoting everything from Hair Oil, Search Services, Banking services, Cement, Gold Jewellery, Gold Loans and what not. No wonder He's referred to as the actor of the century.

In my opinion there isn't a better example of the power of Compounding in Real Life.

The son of the **Harivanshrai Bachchan** a famous Hindi Poet, born in Allahabad, he used to work as a freight broker for a shipping firm in Calcutta.

We all love his voice but you would be surprised to know, that he auditioned for a voice test at All India Radio but was rejected. His height 6feet 3 inches, for which he is appreciated now was considered his liability and none of the lead heroines in those days, wanted to work with him.

He got his first break in 1969 with the movie **Saat Hindustani which didn't do too well,** for which he even won the national award but to get another role he had to struggle for two years.

His role as an angry young man in 1972's *Zanjeer* made him an action movie star. The late seventies and early 80s belonged to him, he appeared in more than 100 films where he worked in many blockbusters like Trishul, Deewar, *Laawaris, Coolie, Naseeb, Silsila,* Muqaddar ka Sikandar, *Shaarabi* underdirectors like Manmohan Desai, Prakash Mehra, Yash Chopra and others.

Then Tragedy struck in 1982 when Amitabh had a near death experience, the doctors and his family had lost hopes after he met with an accident on the sets of the movie Coolie from which he thankfully recovered to become a superstar again for the coming few years.

In 1984 due to his close association with Congress he tried his hand in politics, he got elected as member of Parliament, but soon he realized that it was not to his liking and promised himself that he was never coming back to politics again.

By the 1990s, the limelight surrounding Bachchan had begun to fade and that is when he decided to start his own entertainment production company, Amitabh Bachchan Corporation Limited, and make himself CEO, This is when his movies flopped and he faced a major financial crisis in his life where he lost almost everything he had.

Then Kaun Banega Crorepati happened in 2000, and he climbed his way back up to stardom as an anchor of the extremely popular TV Show and as a film actor, earning additional Filmfare and International Film Award nominations for his work on films like *Baghban* (2003), *Khakee* (2004) and *Paa* (2009).

His hard work and determination have worked for him, he kept on doing what he could to the best of his ability, Regularly.

Even as I am completing this chapter there's an announcement that he has been conferred the prestigious DadaSaheb Phlake award 2019

For someone with all the health issues he has and what he has been through, this is indeed remarkable. At his age, He is one of the highest paid actors in the film industry today, and the most sought after for ads of various products and services.

COMPOUNDING IS THE 8TH WONDER

COMPOUNDING IS POWERFUL COMPOUNDING TAKES TIME

RAJNIKANTH

"Do it for the people who want to see you fail."

– Rajnikanth

"You won't get anything without hard work. What you get without hard work will never fructify."

– Rajinikanth

The second highest paid actor in Asia, Rajnikant is the biggest superstar, the craze on the day his film gets released has to be seen to be believed. Every film release of his, is like a festival for his fans, the day his movie releases, a holiday is declared!

Even today at age 69 he is the lead actor in his movies and his fans cannot have enough of him

Born Shivaji Rao Gaikwad in Bangalore on December 12, 1950, with truly humble beginnings, he lived his life in poverty, his father, a police constable had a meagre income and could not earn enough to take care of all the members of his family.

After completing his schooling, Rajnikanth did jobs such as a carpenter and collie before getting into transport service as a conductor for the Bangalore Transport Service (BTS).

Rajnikant always had a great interest in sports and in acting, he joined the Madras Film Institute and its there during one of his stage plays, he met director K Balachander, who offered him a role in his forthcoming Tamil film. The director suggested that he learn to speak Tamil, which quickly did and went on to master the language.

In 1975, when Rajnikanth made his big-screen debut in Apoorva Raagangal, he had a very small role to play, this helped him bag many roles over the next two years, until he was finally cast in a lead role in the Telugu film *ChilakammaCheppindi*, directed by S P Muthuraman.

In 1978, Rajinikanth had 20 releases across 3 languages, Tamil, Telugu and Kannada!

By the 1990s, Rajinikanth established himself as an entertainer and a star, Almost all the films released during this period were highly successful at the box office.

With many successful hits like *Baasha*(1995), *Muthu* (1995) and *Padayappa*(1999), under his belt, his much-hyped movie *Baba*, co-starring actress Manisha Koirala, failed miserably at the box office in 2002.Critics remarked that it was the end and that "gold does not glitter anymore."

He personally repaid the losses of by the distributors of the movie and three years later, he came up with P Vasu's *Chandramukhi*, which up until 2007 was the longest-running Tamil film of all time.

In 2007, he was paid Rs 26 crore for his role in Sivaji, which made him the highest-paid actor in Asia after Jackie Chan. However In 2008, another movie he starred in -- Kuselan Failed miserably.

In 2019, Rajinikanth starred in Karthik Subbaraj's Movie, *Petta*, in which his performance received praise for his return to his vintage stereotypical style of acting. The combined gross earnings of 3 of his films, *Kaala*, *2.0* and *Petta* by the end of January 2019 was determined to be over ₹1000 crore

As of 2019, Rajinikanth has won six Tamil Nadu State Film Awards—four Best Actor Awards and two Special Awards for Best Actor—and a Filmfare Best Tamil Actor Award. In addition to acting, he has also worked as a producer and screenwriter.

The Government of India has honoured him with the Padma Bhushan (2000) and the Padma Vibhushan (2016). At the 45th International Film Festival of India (2014), he was conferred with the "Centenary Award for Indian Film Personality of the Year"

Rajinikanth is also the only Indian actor to be featured in the Central Board of Secondary Education (CBSE) syllabus, in a lesson titled *From Bus Conductor to Superstar*

Rajinikanth received over 210,000 followers within 24 hours, when he first announced his handle on Twitter, in 2014, which according to *The Economic Times* was deemed by social media research firms as the fastest rate of followers for any Indian celebrity, as well as among the top-10 in the world

There cannot be a better example of the Power of Compounding

COMPOUNDING IS POWERFUL,
COMPOUNDING TAKES TIME

DHIRUBHAI AMBANI

*"If you don't build your dream,
someone else will hire you to build theirs."*

—Dhirubhai Ambani

*"Think Big, Think Fast, Think Ahead,
Ideas are no one's Monopoly."*

—Dhirubhai Ambani

Dhirubhai Ambani, the Founder of Indian Multinational Reliance Industries, was the first Indian entrepreneur to have had his company listed under Forbes 500.

Dhirubhai was born into a middle-class family, his father was a school teacher, he was the third child of five, when Ambani was in school he used to sell "Bhajias"

At the age of 16 he moved to Yemen and worked there as a gas station attendant and clerk in an oil company. It was here that he learnt accounting, book keeping and preparing shipping papers and documents. He also acquired the skill of dealing with banks and insurance companies.

In 1957, Dhirubhai arrived in Mumbai after spending 8 years in Aden (Yemen), at that time he had only Rs 500 in his pocket.

Since he did not have a lot of money to make large investments, he settled as a spice trader under the name Reliance Commercial Corporations. He soon shifted focus to yarn trading, which though had high levels of risks involved, promised richer dividends as well. Starting on a small scale, he soon made big deals in yarn to the point of being elected a director of the Bombay Yarn Merchants Association.

In 1966 he set up a textile mill in Naroda, Ahmedabad. In Jan 1967, production of the finest quality of Nylon began but the companyhad no buyers as the wholesalers refused to buy fabric from Reliance at the instance of established big mill owners. He then personally stepped out on the road and started selling his stock directly to retailers. His daring attitude impressed all and soon the market for 'Vimal', the name of his fabric, grew and started expanding. In no time, it became the finest, best-selling fashion fabric of its times.

By 1972, Reliance became huge and Three years later, it received a nod of excellence from the World Bank. In 1977, Reliance Industries went public and raised equity capital from 58,000 investors, many of them located in small towns.

By 1976-77, Reliance had an annual turnover of Rs 70 crore (Rs 700 million)

Dhirubhai Ambani had his rivals and they tried to bring him down in every way possible, But he survived all that – despite suffering a stroke in 1986, Reliance Industries continued to grow. In the 1990s he turned aggressively toward petrochemicals, oil refining, telecommunications and financial services. **When he breathed his last in 2002 – he was ranked by Forbes as the world's 138th-richest person, with an estimated net worth of $2.9 billion.**

In 2016, he was posthumously honoured with the Padma Vibhushan, India's second highest civilian honour for his contributions to trade and industry.

There can be no better example of the power of compounding where a person arrives with 500 Rs in a new city and at the time of his death is worth 2.9 Billion $

COMPOUNDING IS POWERFUL
COMPOUNDING TAKES TIME

HENRY FORD

> "*If you think you can do a thing or think you can't, You're Right.*"
>
> —Henry Ford

> "*Failure is simply the opportunity to begin again, this time more intelligently.*"
>
> —Henry Ford

Henry Ford, was the founder of the Ford Motor Company, which is one of the most successful automotive companies of all time. However, what many do not know is that Ford failed many times before, in his life, which resulted in two bankruptcies, prior to achieving success.

When we think about Ford, we don't picture the failures because all it took was just succeeding one time. However, in 1899, at the age of 36 years old, Ford formed his first company, the Detroit Automobile Company with backing from the famed lumber baron, William H. Murphy, that company went bankrupt.

His second attempt was in 1901, when he formed the Henry Ford Company, which he ended up leaving with the rights to his name. That company was later renamed to the Cadillac Automobile Company. However, it was Ford's third try, with the Ford Motor Company, that went on to become a huge success.

Ford revolutionized the automobile industry, pioneering not only the Model T and the assembly line, but also the concept and notion of an automobile in every home. Driving became a "thing," and subsequently, Ford's Model T went on to sell over 17 million units.

Ford tried to launch a political career, but never succeeded.

J K ROWLING

"Some Failure in life is inevitable. It is impossible to live without failing at something, unless you live so cautiously that you might as well have not lived at all, in which case you fail by default."

—J K Rowling

In August 1994, Joanne Rowling, a single mother, who was broke and depressed after divorcing her husband after just 1 year of marriage, was writing a novel while studying.

A few years earlier, her mother died from multiple sclerosis, her relationship with her father had broken down and she had suffered a miscarriage.

In 1995 after finishing her script, she approached 12 major publishers, however all 12 major publishers rejected the *Harry Potter* script. But, a year later when a small publishing house, Bloomsbury, accepted it and extended a very small £1500 advance. In 1997, the book was published with only 1000 copies, 500 of which were distributed to libraries.

In 1997 and 1998, the book won awards from Nestle Smarties Book Prize and the British Book Award for Children's Book of the Year. In the next five years, Rowling's novel broke book all sales records in the U.S. and U.K., and she went on to sell her book rights for a film to Warner Bros for a seven figure Sum.

The Harry Potter book series became the best-selling book series of all-time—over 500 million copies sold worldwide—and Rowling became the world's first billionaire author.

Another example of the Power of Compounding

COMPOUNDING IS POWERFUL
COMPOUNDING TAKES TIME

WALT DISNEY

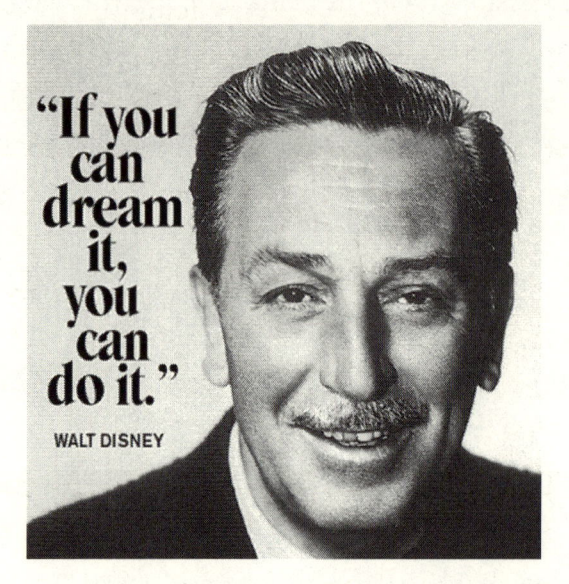

> "I think it's important to have a good hard failure when you're young... Because it makes you kind of aware of what can happen to you. Because of it I've never had any fear in my whole life when we've been near collapse and all of that. I've never been afraid."
>
> —Walt Disney

"If you can dream it, you can do it."
WALT DISNEY

Walt Disney was considered a failure; He was fired by the editor in 1919 from his job at the Kansas City Star paper because he "lacked imagination and had no good ideas." However, the man who brought us Mickey Mouse and a slew of other characters didn't stop failing there.

Disney started as an apprentice at a Kansas City commercial art studio. and later he and his older brother

Roy launched their own cartoon business, Laugh-O-Gram Studios, in 1920, but the company went bankrupt a couple years later.

He then went and tried his hand at acting and failed at that too.

Noticing there weren't any animations studios in California, Disney and his brother Roy started an animation studio. Not so long after, Disney found his first major success with the creation of Oswald the Lucky Rabbit, but Disney found his luck had run out. He discovered that his producer had taken his team of animators from under him and that he no longer had any legal rights to Oswald the Lucky Rabbit.

The early failures in Disney's life didn't dissuade him from moving forward.

Instead of fighting the loss or plotting his revenge, Disney decided to walk away and start over again. It was on the train ride back to California that he created Mickey Mouse. But it wasn't easy. Bankers rejected the concept of his famous mouse over 300 times before one said yes

Even with the success of Mickey Mouse, Disney still faced challenges in keeping his business afloat. He was overworked, which led to Disney having a nervous breakdown.

After taking some time off to recover he worked on a full length animation feature, *Snow White and the Seven Dwarfs* (1937) which went on to become a huge success at the box office, but the films that followed *Pinocchio* (1940), *Fantasia* (1940) and *Bambi* (1942) ended up as failures.

However, it also laid the foundation for a successful career. When he formed the Walt Disney Company, all of his past failures helped to pave the way for a successful business.

Disney and the Walt Disney Company have touched the lives of millions across the globe. From cartoons, to theme parks, and animated movies, both children and adults now enjoy the fruits of Disney's labour. Had he given up; things would have been far different. But he persevered, even through bankruptcy.

COLONEL SANDERS

For many of us, experiencing two or three rejections can be disheartening. **Imagine how it must have been for Harland David Sanders, whose fried chicken recipe was rejected over 1,000 times.**

When Sanders was 65 years old, he found himself bankrupt after his restaurant business had failed.

He drove around in his car, pleading with diner and restaurant owners to use his fried chicken recipe. The deal was that for every piece of chicken sold, they were to give him a nickel as a commission.

He was turned down 1,009 times before a restaurant agreed to use his recipe, which he called Kentucky Fried Chicken.

Today, Colonel Sanders is an iconic figure representing one of the tastiest fried chickens in the world. People know him because of his iconic white suit and bow tie. Colonel Sanders was the founder of Kentucky Fried Chicken (KFC). Sanders got off to a rocky start in life. In fact, it wasn't until the age of 62 that he set out with a $105 social security check in hand to pitch his chicken recipe to restaurants. 1,009 folks told him he was crazy, but he didn't give up.

Sanders worked many jobs including fireman, tire salesman, insurance salesman, and of course, a cook. He brewed up his secret chicken recipe between 1939-1940 when he figured out how to pressure fry the chicken in a faster and more consistent product all the time. He was at the age of 50 when that happened.

However, it wasn't until 1952 that he hit the road and began trying to sell his franchise-model chicken restaurant. The first restaurant that he landed was based out of Salt Lake City, Utah, which became the first Kentucky Fried Chicken. The restaurant tripled its sales within a year where 75% of that revenue was from the colonel's chicken.

The company grew and expanded faster than he could have ever imagined. In 1964, at the age of 74 years old, Sanders sold the company for $2 million dollars to a group of investors led by Jack C. Massey and John Y. Brown Jr. He retained the rights to the Canadian franchises and stayed on as a salaried goodwill ambassador to the company.

However, this just goes to show you that it doesn't matter how old you are or just how much money you have to your name in order to accomplish something great.

COMPOUNDING IS POWERFUL,
COMPOUNDING TAKES TIME

ABRAHAM LINCOLN

"I am a slow walker, but I never walk back."

—*Abraham Lincoln*

"The best way to predict your future is to create it."

—*Abraham Lincoln*

Born in 1809, Abraham Lincoln was the 16th President of the United States. But he failed numerous times before attaining the highest office in the land.

Lincoln's failures were broad and numerous. He achieved the unique feat of leaving for a war a captain and returning a private (the lowest military rank)

In 1832, when he was 23-years old, Lincoln lost his job. At the same time, he also lost his bid for State Legislature.

Just 3 years later, at the age of 26, the love of his life, Ann Rutledge died. Another three years later, He lost his bid to become Speaker in the Illinois House of Representatives.

In 1848, at the age of 39-years, He failed in his bid to become Commissioner of the General Land Office in D.C. Ten years after that, at the age of 49-years old, he was defeated in his quest to become a U.S. Senator. Of course, through all the personal, business and political failures, Lincoln didn't give up. In 1846, Lincoln was elected to the U.S. House of Representatives where he drafted a bill to abolish slavery. In 1861, at the age of 52, he secured the office of President of the United States.

Another example of the Power of Compounding

COMPOUNDING IS POWERFUL,
COMPOUNDING TAKES TIME

THOMAS EDISON

"Our greatest weakness lies in giving up. The most certain way to succeed is always to try just one more time."

—*Thomas Edison*

"Genius is one percent inspiration and ninety-nine percent perspiration."

—*Thomas Edison*

Thomas Edison may be the greatest inventor in history. He is credited with Inventing many useful items including the phonograph and a practical light bulb.

Thomas Edison was born in Milan, Ohio on February 11, 1847, he did not do well in school, his teachers said he was "too stupid to learn anything," he was partially deaf and ended up being home schooled by his mother.

As a child he was selling vegetables, candy and newspapers on trains. One day he saved a child from a runaway train. The child's father repaid Edison by training him as a telegraph operator. As a telegraph operator, Thomas became interested in communications. He set up his first lab in his parent's basement at the age of 10.

Edison did not look for problems in need of solutions; he looked for solutions in need of modification.

In 1877, at the age of 30-years old, Edison invented the phonograph,

In 1878, just a year later, Edison began working on the incandescent lightbulb, Edison did not actually invent the light bulb, other inventors much before him had already demonstrated and patented versions of incandescent lights, he set out to do something he called perfecting—finding ways to make things better or cheaper or both, he wanted to make a commercially-viable incandescent lightbulb that would be both long-lasting and highly efficient by not drawing too much energy to operate

He actually failed over 10,000 times trying to make it commercially viable,

When asked by a reporter what he felt after so many failed attempts. He said, *"I have not failed 10,000 times. I have not failed once. I have succeeded in proving that those 10,000 ways will not work. When I have eliminated the ways that will not work, I will find the way that will work."*

He suffered through not succeeding numerous times, but where others quit, he persisted.

On a single day in 1888, he wrote down a hundred and twelve ideas!

In addition to the light bulb and the phonograph, he is also credited with inventing the kinetoscope, the dictating machine, the alkaline battery, the electric meter, a talking doll, the world's largest rock crusher, an electric pen, a fruit preserver, and a tornado-proof house.

However, not all his inventions worked or made money. His work in a number of fields created the basis for much of the technologies that we enjoy today and take for granted

Edison had 1,093 patents to his name at the time of his death

Edison is a classic example of the Power of Compounding

COMPOUNDING IS POWERFUL, COMPOUNDING TAKES TIME

MICHAEL JORDAN

> "I've always believed that if you put in the work, the results will come."
>
> —*Michael Jordan*

Michael Jordan is a former professional basketball player, He is called "the greatest basketball player of all time,"

When he was 15-years old, sin high school, Jordan was passed up for the varsity basketball team, instead being assigned to the junior varsity team. He cried after he saw that list without his name on it. But instead of giving up, his mom convinced him to push forward. Every time he thought about stopping his training, he would picture that list without his name on it.

He took failure in his stride and pushed himself harder. In his first season at North Carolina he was named

Atlantic Coast Conference (ACC) Rookie of the Year for 1982. Jordan was a member of the Summer 1984 United States Olympic basketball team that won the gold medal in Los Angeles, California

At the age of 21-years old, he entered the NBA as a professional basketball player for the Chicago Bulls, where he would go on to win six championship titles

A broken foot made him miss 64 games during the 1985–86 season, but returned soon to prove that he was the best in the game. In what is still considered the greatest game in NBA history, he set the still-unbroken record of 63 ppg (points per game) against the Boston Celtics team

In 1993 he announced his first retirement only to come back in 1994-1995

In 1997 he was ranked the world's highest paid athlete, with a $30 million contract—the largest one-year salary in sports history—and approximately $40 million a year in endorsement fees.

He retired for a second time in 1999 and his retirement was called the end of an era

In September 2001, Jordan announced that he was ending his three-year retirement to play again at age thirty-eight.

His best-known quote is

I have missed more than 9,000 shots in my career. I have lost almost 300 games. On 26 occasions I have been

entrusted to take the game winning shot, and I missed. I have failed over and over and over again in my life. And that is why I succeeded - MICHAEL JORDAN

MICHEAL JORDAN clearly is an Example of the Power of Compounding

Compounding is Powerful,

Compounding Takes Time.

WILLIAM AND ORVILLE WRIGHT

Wilbur and Orville Wright were the pioneers of aviation, The2 brothers changed the way we travel, and their efforts and struggles serve as an inspiration and symbol for soaring to great heights.

Neither Wilbur nor Orville attended college.

Starting out with printing a weekly newspaper, they began repairing and selling bicycles,To augment the inctome from their printing trade.

from 1899 to 1905for 6-yearsthey began with designing a simple model glider, which Wilbur Wright flew as a kite...and ended with the development of the first practical airplane, the Wright Flyer III

Their main goal was to create a flying machine that stayed up in the air for a sustained period of time. They put in countless hours to create prototypes, and many of them didn't work as intended, crashing on the sand at Kitty Hawk, North Carolina. Those crashes led to the creation of better versions of the brothers' flying machine, until that day in December 1903, when Wilbur was able to sustain powered flight for more than 10 seconds.

For two years they made flight after flight, fine tuning everything from the propeller to the engine to controls. At first, they could only fly in a straight line for less than a minute. But by the end of 1905, they were able to fly in loops, staying in flight for over half an hour. The 1905 Wright Flyer was the world's first *practical* airplane. The world would never be the same again.

The life and times of the Wright Brothers is a classic example of the Power of compounding

COMPOUNDING IS POWERFUL
COMPOUNDING TAKES TIME

JACK MA

"Never give up today is hard, tomorrow will be worse, but the day after tomorrow will be sunshine."

—Jack Ma

Jack Ma is the founder of the E-commerce company ALIBABA, and is the **richest man in China** with an estimated **net worth of $39 Billion**

In his early childhood, Jack Ma Failed in his Primary School examinations, Twice!

He Failed Thrice during his Middle School exams.

He taught himself English at age 12.

He failed at the entrance exams thrice, when applying to universities!

He even applied and wrote to Harvard University ten times about being admitted – and got rejected each time.

After getting his Bachelor's degree, Jack tried many times but he failed to get a job!

He often gives this example

"When KFC came to China, 24 people went for the job. Twenty-three people were accepted. I was the only guy who wasn't"

He also one of the 5 applicants to a job in Police force and was the only one getting rejected after being told, "No, you're no good"

He finally got a job teaching English at a local university. Yet when he discovered the internet in 1995 while visiting a friend in the United States, he saw an opportunity to bring the world wide web to China.

He managed to convince 17 of his friends to invest and join him in his new e-commerce start-up – Alibaba, a company which he began from his apartment. He created Alibaba from scratch and went on to become one of the richest men in the world.

COMPOUNDING IS POWERFUL
COMPOUNDING TAKES TIME

Made in the USA
Columbia, SC
30 September 2021